ALL ABOUT YOUR 401k PLAN

SIMPLE ANSWERS TO SECURING YOUR FINANCIAL FUTURE

Ellie Williams Clinton
Diane Pearl

PROBUS PUBLISHING

Chicago, Illinois
Cambridge, England

9-7-95

ISBN 1-55738-805-9

Printed in the United States of America

BB

1 2 3 4 5 6 7 8 9 0

TAQ/BJS

Table of Contents

Acknowledgments

Thanks to the many U.S. companies and organizations who have given their employees the opportunity to take control of their retirement through 401(k) and 403(b) plans.

Special thanks for their ideas and support goes to the *MONEYWISE* Advisory Board: Craig Campbell, Eleanor Fry, Judy Jones, Cindy Lander, and Brainerd LaTourette III.

As always, thanks to our families, and to Linda Bryant, founding partner of *MONEYWISE.*

Introduction

Patty is a thirty-something, single mother who works two jobs supporting her three small children, just making ends meet. She saves what she can to provide an emergency cushion and works hard to invest small amounts.

Mike and Leslie are in their early forties; they have a family, a mortgage, two car payments, and moderate savings accounts. They expect to use most of their savings for their children's college educations, weddings, and the commendable but expensive possibility of graduate degrees.

Julie and Marty are in their mid-fifties; Marty makes a good living in a Fortune 500 corporation, and Julie is a homemaker. They have begun to save for retirement and have just realized how expensive it will be to support their lifestyle.

Do these families have anything in common financially? At first glance, the answer might be, "Not much," but after a closer look, there is one not-so-glaring similarity: All of them need to prepare for retirement. No matter what happens to our Social Security system (more on that later) it will not fully support Patty, Mike and Leslie, or Julie and Marty. Chances are, company pension plans will not take up the slack, either. So, while each is in a very different financial situation, all of these families have not a moment to lose in making sure that they will have enough money to be comfortable in retirement.

Only you can ensure that the money will be there when you need it. If you are one of the millions of people in this country who are eligible for a 401(k) or 403(b) retirement plan, you have the means to control your financial future. Of course, there are pros and cons to investing in such plans, and we will discuss both sides of the issue. Fortunately, there are countless opportunities in the investment world from which to choose. The key to developing a winning strategy is knowing your options and taking full advantage of them.

This book will explain what those options are, what you should consider in making a financial decision, and where to get the best information. The biggest mistakes you can make are assuming that retirement planning is only for "older" people and letting someone else manage your money without evaluating their performance. At *MONEYWISE*, we believe that no one will watch your money like you will. We have written this book not to convince you to invest in your retirement plan, but to give you the best information to make that decision yourself.

Because our backgrounds are in banking and brokerage, we know what salespeople may try to sell you (we've been there) and what you should find out before spending your hard-earned dollars. Ellie Williams Clinton graduated *summa cum laude* in Finance from the University of Missouri-Columbia. She has 10 years of banking and brokerage experience and managed a St. Louis brokerage firm. She is an experienced investment adviser and holds six securities licenses.

Diane Pearl graduated with an Associate of Science degree from Lake Land College in Mattoon, Illinois. As investment club director for a St. Louis bank, she provided training and education for many investment clubs. She acquired her interest in financial education during her years as a securities broker; she holds four securities licenses.

MONEYWISE is a St. Louis-based financial training and education firm, dedicated to teaching people the right questions to ask and to helping them make educated financial decisions.

In addition to working with individuals, *MONEY-WISE* provides educational programs through the workplace to teach employees how to make the most of their paychecks and how to make company benefit plans work for them.

Other books by *MONEYWISE* are *99 Great Answers to Everyone's Investment Questions* (co-authored by Linda Bryant) and *The Smart Woman's Guide to Spending, Saving, and Managing Money.*

All About Your 401(k) Plan is not intended to advise you on specific investment choices or tax strategies. We advocate using professionals, reading books and magazines, and taking financial courses taught by impartial instructors before taking action. Our goal is to educate and inform you, to enable you to make successful financial decisions now and in the future.

Whether you have purchased this book yourself or received it from your employer, we hope that you will use its information to keep more of the money you make.

Chapter One

The Inside Story on 401(k) and 403(b) Plans

I work 40 hours a week and don't have time to be a financial expert ... There are too many choices in my plan and I don't understand ANY of them ... I just don't know where to begin ... I'll worry about retirement later ... I can't afford to make 401(k) contributions right now ... I'll deal with it in the next enrollment period ... I hate to make financial decisions, they give me headaches.

Do any of these statements sound familiar? When it comes to your future, don't let excuses get in the way of your financial well-being. The fact is that fewer and fewer employers can shoulder the financial risks and responsibilities of traditional pension plans. By providing 401(k) plans in place of, or in addition to, a pension, they allow you, the employee, the opportunity to control your financial future. Willing or not, you become your own pension manager—and you can learn how to do it with confidence.

What Exactly Is a 401(k) Plan?

Let's start with the name, which sounds very technical. Could there possibly be 401 different things you have to know about this plan? Good news. 401(k) is simply the section of the Internal Revenue Service code that allows

1

the existence of this particular type of retirement plan. We'll spare you the legal definition and start by explaining how a 401(k) plan works and what the advantages and disadvantages are to investing your money in one.

How does a 401(k) plan work?

A 401(k) plan allows your employer to deduct a specified amount from your paycheck to be invested in an account for your retirement. You choose the percentage of your gross income to be deducted each pay period and whether you want it invested before or after taxes. Generally, your plan will allow you to change that percentage periodically.

After it is deducted, your employer transmits your money to a custodian (a bank or trust company) who deposits it into an account in your name. All amounts that have been deducted from your salary legally belong to you, and changes in your employer's retirement plan or in the status of your employment cannot affect the money you have deposited.

Once the money reaches your account, it is invested in the manner you choose. You may invest your money in any of the options offered through the plan, and you may even split your investments, for example, 50 percent in one choice and 50 percent in another. Just as you can change the amount you deduct, you also have the ability to change your mind about your investment choices periodically. Don't worry about making a mistake—the biggest mistake you can make is doing nothing. With time, practice, and continued learning, your decisions will come easier and your confidence will build.

Now that you know the mechanics, let's look at the advantages and disadvantages of investing your money in a 401(k) plan.

Advantages of a 401(k) plan

1) Tax deductibility: The amount you contribute to a 401(k) plan is deducted from your gross income before federal and state taxes are computed. (The wage base for computing FICA taxes does not exclude your contributions.) This means you do not pay any income tax on the amount contributed until you withdraw it from the account. For example, if you earn $40,000 per year and elect to contribute 10 percent ($4,000) of your salary to your 401(k) plan, you declare only $36,000 ($40,000 – $4,000) of taxable income for the year. Let's take a look at the difference in the money you keep when you invest in a 401(k) plan, in Tables 1-1, 1-2, 1-3, and 1-4.

$$ Note: State income taxes, if they apply to you, make the difference even more striking because your state taxes will be reduced as well.

2) Tax deferral on investment growth: With ordinary investments, which are not part of a 401(k) or individual retirement account (IRA), capital gains and interest or

Table 1-1   Contributing to a 401(k) Plan

Single, No Dependents	Before Contribution	During Contribution
Annual gross salary	$15,000	$15,000
6 percent contribution	0	900
Net salary	15,000	14,100
Federal withholding	1,794	1,716
FICA/Medicare (doesn't change)	1,148	1,148
Take-home pay	12,058	11,236
Contribution to savings		900
The money you keep	**12,058**	**12,136**

Table 1-2   Contributing to a 401(k) Plan

Single, No Dependents	Before Contribution	During Contribution
Gross salary	$25,000	$25,000
6 percent contribution	0	1,500
Net salary	25,000	23,500
Federal withholding	3,354	3,120
FICA/Medicare (doesn't change)	1,913	1,913
Take-home pay	19,733	18,467
Contribution to savings		1,500
The money you keep	**19,733**	**19,967**

Table 1-3   Contributing to a 401(k) Plan

Single, No Dependents	Before Contribution	During Contribution
Gross salary	$50,000	$50,000
6 percent contribution	0	3,000
Net salary	50,000	47,000
Federal withholding	10,244	9,360
FICA/Medicare (doesn't change)	3,825	3,825
Take-home pay	35,931	33,815
Contribution to savings		3,000
The money you keep	**35,931**	**36,815**

dividends are taxed in the year in which they are earned. (Capital gains are incurred when you sell an investment for an amount higher than your purchase price. Interest and dividends are the periodic earnings of your investment.) With a 401(k) plan you do not pay any income tax on the growth or earnings of investments held in the plan until you withdraw your money. This allows you to use

Table 1-4   Contributing to a 401(k) Plan

Single, No Dependents	Before Contribution	During Contribution
Gross salary	$75,000	$75,000
6 percent contribution	0	4,500
Net salary	75,000	70,500
Federal withholding	17,804	16,409
FICA/Medicare (doesn't change)	4,808	4,808
Take-home pay	52,388	49,283
Contribution to savings		4,500
The money you keep	**52,388**	**53,783**

money, which would have been paid to the IRS in taxes, to earn more money for you. Table 1-5 shows how a single investment of $2,000 can grow to $6,712 in a 401(k) after 20 years. In an ordinary, taxable investment, the same $2,000 would grow to only $4,414, a difference of $2,298.

$$ *Note:* Unless otherwise stated, all 401(k) elective contributions discussed are considered to be pre-tax contributions.

Table 1-5   A Single Contribution of $2,000

	Ordinary Investment	401(k) Investment
Investable income	$2,000	$2,000
Current income taxes paid at 28%	560	0
Funds available to invest after taxes	1,440	2,000
Value after 20 years earning 8% (ordinary investment income taxed at 28 percent annually)	4,414	9,322
Taxes due on 401(k) withdrawal at 28%	0	2,610
Money you keep after 20 years	**4,414**	**6,712**

Table 1-6 shows how 20 years of annual contributions of $2,000 can grow to either $54,598 or $71,169, depending on the type of account you choose. The difference of $16,571 is not small change.

Table 1-7 shows how important it is to begin saving early. A 25-year-old can accumulate nearly $1 million for retirement by investing $2,000 each year in an account that earns 10 percent.

3) Convenience: Your retirement savings contribution is deducted directly from your paycheck, before you get a chance to spend it. Do you ever have those months where you just don't know where the money went? Or, have you

Table 1-6   Annual Contributions of $2,000

	Ordinary Investment	401(k) Investment
investable income	$2,000	$2,000
Current income taxes paid at 28%	560	0
Funds available to invest after taxes	1,440	2,000
Value after 20 years earning 8% (ordinary investment income taxed at 28 percent annually)	54,598	98,846
Taxes due on 401(k) withdrawal at 28%	0	27,677
Money you keep after 20 years	**54,598**	**71,169**

Table 1-7   Invest $2,000 each year in a 401(k) How much will you have at 65?

Beginning Age	5% Return	10% Return	15% Return
25	$253,680	$973,704	$4,191,908
35	139,522	361,887	999,914
45	69,439	126,005	235,620
55	26,414	35,062	46,699

created a budget, which shows plenty left over after expenses, but real life just doesn't seem to work the same way? Having your contributions deducted from your paycheck makes saving for retirement easy and relatively painless.

401(k) Tip: Always pay yourself first, in both a 401(k) plan *and* in additional savings. You can then be assured that *you* get paid. Let the other bills fight for what's left over.

---

4) Discipline: You cannot withdraw the money invested in a 401(k) plan before age 59½ without paying a 10 percent penalty to the IRS. While we will also list this as a disadvantage, there is a bright side for those who have trouble saving. If ordinary savings accounts are just too tempting, you may find that the best way to save (and not spend the money as soon as you have saved it) is through an account that has a stiff penalty for pre-retirement withdrawals.

401(k) Tip: Don't even consider your 401(k) account when you are looking for ready cash. Lock it up and throw away the key until you reach retirement.

---

5) High investable amounts: By law, you can save up to a maximum pre-tax contribution of $9,240 (1994 rules) in your 401(k) plan. The maximum combined employee and employer contribution is the lesser of $30,000 or 25 percent of your annual compensation. This compares to a maximum annual IRA contribution of $2,000. Keep in mind that you may reach your maximum well before the IRS limit, due to your plan limits. For example, if your plan allows you to contribute a maximum of 10 percent of your $30,000 salary, the most you can contribute to your 401(k) account each year is $3,000, not $9,240. If your employer matches 50 percent ($1,500) of your contributions, the upper limit to your combined deposits is $4,500, not $30,000. In any case, you have the ability to save more for retirement through your 401(k) plan than in any ordinary IRA, and as your income grows, so will the amounts that you can contribute.

6) Dollar-cost-averaging: Investing a regular amount at periodic intervals takes the emotion out of investing. With a consistent plan, you continue to buy shares when markets are low (probably the best time to invest, but psychologically the most difficult) and you do not jump in head-first when sentiments are high (and markets may be near their peaks). By investing a constant amount, you will buy more shares when prices are low and fewer shares when prices are high, resulting in a lower average cost per share. See Table 1-8 for a numerical demonstration of dollar-cost-averaging.

7) Mobility: If you leave your current employer, you have several options that will allow you to maintain your retirement account. If your new employer has a 401(k) plan and will allow you to transfer deposits from your previous plan into it, you may request that your current custodian send your funds directly to the custodian of your new plan. If you would prefer to have control of the funds and unlimited investment opportunities, you may open a self-directed IRA with a bank, brokerage firm, or mutual fund company and have the funds transferred directly to your new investment company. In either case, the direct trans-

Table 1-8   Dollar-Cost-Averaging

Month	Regular Investment	Share Price	Shares Purchased*
January	$200	$10	20.00
February	$200	$10	20.00
March	$200	$9	22.22
April	$200	$8	25.00
May	$200	$8	25.00
June	$200	$8	25.00
July	$200	$9	22.22
August	$200	$9	22.22
September	$200	$10	20.00
October	$200	$11	18.18
November	$200	$10	20.00
December	$200	$11	18.18
Total	$2,400	$113	258.02

Average share price over time period = 113/12 = $9.42.

Average cost of shares purchased = $2,400/258.02 = $8.42.

*Assumes fractional mutual fund share purchases.

fer will provide your funds with continuous custodial care, preventing any sort of tax liability. If you are younger than 59½ and your current custodian sends the funds to you, you have 60 days to reinvest the money in an IRA in order to avoid penalty. (You may be subject to federal income tax withholding, so see Chapter 9 for more specifics on transfers and rollovers.)

Disadvantages of a 401(k) plan

While the benefits of a 401(k) plan are many, there are several reasons to look before you leap.

1) Lack of liquidity: If you withdraw the funds in your 401(k) plan before you reach age 59½, two things happen:

◆ You must pay a 10 percent IRS penalty on the dollar amount withdrawn.

◆ You must pay ordinary income tax on the dollar amount withdrawn.

For these reasons, 401(k) plans are strictly designed to accumulate retirement savings. Do not invest every available dollar into your plan without creating separate investment accounts for emergencies (we recommend three to six months' living expenses) or for other non-retirement needs, such as college education costs or a down payment for a house.

2) Limited investment choices: A small plan may offer only limited investment options. Plans vary—some allow you to invest in many different mutual funds, some just a few. If you have only a few options and are not particularly impressed with their investment performance, you may feel that, even considering the tax advantages, your money could work harder for you outside the 401(k) plan.

3) The possibility that personal income taxes will rise drastically: Some people feel that even if their income will be lower, tax rates will be higher when they retire and the time to pay Uncle Sam is now. Given the current United States deficit, there lurks the possibility that politicians will choose to reduce the deficit by increasing tax rates on current income. However, because the money that you don't have to pay in taxes now can earn income and grow for you all the years until retirement, income tax rates would have to rise substantially in order to nullify the advantage of current tax deferral. In the example in Table 1-6, the individual's income tax rates would have to rise from 28 percent to 45 percent on the day before withdrawal before the available funds from the tax-deferred account would be equal to the ordinary account.

As you can see, the advantages of participating in a plan generally outweigh the disadvantages, but there are other issues.

Should you invest after-tax funds in your 401(k)?

Most plans give you the option of investing in the traditional pre-tax method or of investing income that has already been taxed. While most participants choose the pre-tax option, some take advantage of after-tax investing, reasoning that their funds are readily available without penalty or additional taxes. They forego the tax advantages in favor of liquidity. If you are trying to decide whether to invest pre- or after-tax, consider the following two rules:

◆ Always take full advantage of tax deductibility and tax deferral for retirement funds.

◆ Avoid investing funds that you will need *before* retirement in pre-tax retirement accounts, which penalize early withdrawal.

So, consider the use of the money you are investing. Choose *pre-tax* for retirement funds and *after-tax* for college educations, homes, and autos. If the convenience and investment performance of your 401(k) plan make it an appealing investment vehicle, consider the after-tax method for your *non-retirement* savings.

403(b) Plans for Teachers and Employees of Tax-exempt Organizations

When we talk to a group about 401(k) plans, the question invariably is asked, "I have a 403(b)—does this same information apply to me?" The answer is, "Generally, yes, with a few differences." While the 403(b) plan may sound like a unique beast, the primary goals and rules of the two plans are the same. The main difference between a 403(b) and a 401(k) plan is the type of company or organization that offers each.

Who is eligible for a 403(b) plan?

Your employer may offer a 403(b) plan if it is a public school or a tax-exempt organization. A public school is defined as an educational organization of a state or local government or any of its agencies or instrumentalities. You are eligible as an employee of a public school if you perform either direct or indirect services for that school. Direct services include those provided by teachers, principals, custodial employees, and administrative employees. Indirect services include jobs which are not performed in the schools, but which are involved in the operation or direction of educational programs for the public schools. Department of Education employees and those elected or appointed to office in the field of education are also eligible.

Tax-exempt organizations, such as religious, charitable, or educational groups, hospital service organizations, or the separate, tax-exempt entities of a government instrumentality are also eligible providers of 403(b) plans.

How do 403(b) plans work?

Just like 401(k) plans, 403(b)s allow your employer to contribute a percentage of your salary to a tax-deductible, tax-
deferred investment plan for your retirement. Wages
contributed to your plan are not included in taxable income for the year in which they are contributed, but are
included in your wage base for computation of FICA
taxes. The restrictions on withdrawal are also the same:

◆ 10 percent penalty for withdrawal before age 59½

◆ Current income tax on any withdrawal

◆ Mandatory withdrawals after age 70½

While 403(b) plans are often called tax-sheltered annuities (TSA) because many plans invest in annuity contracts, your 403(b) plan may invest in mutual funds or
other retirement investments, as do many 401(k) plans.
The availability of other investments depends on your
plan trustee.

Combined annual limits on elective deferrals

Contribution limits generally apply to all employer-provided qualified retirement plans. Elective deferrals are the
total of all contributions to:

◆ 401(k) plans

◆ 501(c)(18) plans

◆ Simplified employee pension (SEP) plans

◆ 403(b) plans /also known as tax-sheltered annuities

A combined limit applies to the total amount that you can defer each year under all of these plans. The limit for 1994 is $9,240, and is increased by a cost-of-living adjustment each year. However, if you are covered by different plans, and one is a tax-sheltered annuity, then the basic limit ($9,240 for 1994) is increased by the amount deferred in the tax-sheltered annuity that year, up to an overall total of $9,500. If you have completed at least 15 years of service with an educational organization, hospital, home health service agency, health and welfare service agency, church, or associated organization, the $9,500 limit is increased each tax year, by the smallest of the following:

◆ $3,000

◆ $15,000, reduced by increases to the $9,500 limit you were allowed in earlier years

◆ $5,000 times the number of your years of service with the organization, minus the total elective deferrals made under the plan for you for earlier years

Cost of insurance protection

If your 403(b) plan invests in annuity contracts, which provide you with incidental life insurance protection, you must include the cost of the insurance in your taxable wages for the year.

Amount payable upon your death	−	Cash value of the contract at year end	=	Current life insurance protection

The one-year cost of term life insurance protection can be figured from an IRS table or from current, published life insurance premium rates of the annuity company used.

Most of the other rules surrounding 403(b) plans are similar to those of 401(k)s. For more specific information, consult your tax adviser, plan document, and IRS Publication 571, *Tax-Sheltered Annuity Programs for Employees of Public Schools and Certain Tax-Exempt Organizations.*

Important Terms

Before you read on, take note of different relevant terms and definitions that will be helpful in understanding the language of 401(k) and 403(b) plans.

Elective contribution: The funds which you direct your employer to withhold from your paycheck and deposit into the plan. You do not pay current income taxes on your contribution. The money belongs to you and may be withdrawn subject to the rules of your plan. If withdrawn you must pay current income taxes and, if withdrawn before age 59½, IRS penalties.

After-tax contribution: Many plans allow you to invest "after-tax" dollars into your plan. These contributions are not deducted from your gross income when computing taxes, but are taxed as any other compensation is. The investment income and growth of these funds do not enjoy the same tax-deferred status as elective contributions, but may be withdrawn without penalty or additional taxes.

Investment option: The investment choice or choices in which you direct your money to be invested. You may be able to choose from well-known mutual funds, from privately managed funds, annuities, or other investment possibilities, such as your company stock.

Matching: At the same time your contribution is deposited, your employer may choose to make a matching deposit in either cash or company stock. Matching is usually expressed as a percent, such as "25 percent matching," which means your employer will deposit $.25 for every $1.00 you contribute, up to a specified amount. For example, at Wilson Trucking, employees may elect to deposit up to 10 percent of their gross pay into the 401(k) plan. Wilson has promised to match $.25 for every employee dollar contributed, up to an election level of 5 percent. Jeff makes $25,000 at Wilson Trucking and has elected to contribute 10 percent of his pay ($2,500) into the plan; each year, Wilson will add $312.50 to his account (see Table 1-9).

401(k) Tip: Company matching funds are "free" money. The $312.50 is an immediate 12.5 percent return on Jeff's $2,500, before the investments have even begun to earn interest or dividends.

Transfer: A transfer, also called a direct transfer, or custodian-to-custodian transfer, is a method of withdrawing your funds from your 401(k) plan and depositing them

Table 1-9

Salary	$25,000
Percent contributed by Jeff	10%
Amount contributed by Jeff	$2,500
Amount used to compute company match	5% maximum = $1,250
Company matching amount	25% of $1,250 = 312.50
Total deposited to Jeff's 401(k) account in one year	$2,812.50

with another custodian. In a transfer, the funds are sent directly to the new custodian and never to you, the participant. The destination may be the custodian of an IRA, 401(k) plan, 403(b) plan, or any other qualified retirement plan. Transferring your account to another custodian prevents you from incurring any tax liability or IRS penalty.

Rollover: A rollover is an alternative method of withdrawing your funds from your plan and reinvesting them with another custodian. In this procedure, the plan participant receives a check for the account value (or the actual stock or investments that were contained in the account) and then remits it to a new custodian. In order to avoid any income taxes or penalty, the funds must be remitted to the new custodian within 60 days of receipt. The IRS currently requires employers to withhold 20 percent of distributions that are paid directly to employees, even if the intent is to roll over the funds. See Chapter 9 for more detail on transfers and rollovers.

Vesting: Your employer has the option of rewarding length of employment by creating a schedule in which matching funds are "vested" after a certain number of years. Vested funds are yours and may be withdrawn, subject to the same restrictions as contributed funds. Funds that are not yet vested cannot be withdrawn. For example, a *three-* to *seven-year vesting* schedule is:

> 20 percent after 3 years,
> 40 percent after 4 years,
> 60 percent after 5 years,
> 80 percent after 6 years,
> 100 percent after 7 or more years,

An individual who had contributed $1,000 and received matching funds of $250, and who then left his employer after three years, would be entitled to withdraw, transfer, or roll over his $1,000 contribution plus 20 percent of the $250 in matching funds. Total available to the employee = $1,050.

In the example of Jeff at Wilson Trucking, the $2,500 Jeff contributed belongs to him, because it came from his paycheck. The $312.50 contributed by Wilson Trucking may or may not belong to him right away.

Loans: Many employers allow you to borrow a portion of your 401(k) account and pay yourself back, with interest. While it is not advisable to use your account for current expenses, in the case of financial emergency it is better to borrow and repay than to withdraw and pay penalties and taxes.

401(k) Dilemma: Susan and Rob, both 35, have about $30,000 in their two 401(k) accounts and are thinking about withdrawing $20,000 to add a room to their house. How will this affect their future?

First, the $20,000 they withdraw will be subject to 10 percent ($2,000) in IRS penalties and, assuming a 28 percent tax bracket, $5,600 in current income taxes. They will net only $12,400 from the $20,000 withdrawal.

Second, the money that they take out will not be growing to provide a secure retirement. At 8 percent, that $20,000 would grow to $201,253 in 30 years. Is an extra room worth *that?*

If they absolutely must have the addition and do not have enough home equity to finance it with a home equity loan, they should plan to *borrow—not* withdraw—the money from their plans.

Under current law, a loan cannot exceed the lesser of $50,000 or one-half of the present value of the employee's vested interest in the plan. An exception is provided for accounts whose value is less than $20,000. The loan maximum in those cases is $10,000. Loans must be repaid within five years, unless they are used to acquire a principal residence. In those cases, the loan may be amortized in equal payments, made not less than quarterly. There may be a loan application charge or a fee for annual maintenance.

In the example of Susan and Rob, they could borrow $15,000 from their plans, which would keep them at the 50 percent borrowing limit. They would have more to spend on the new room ($15,000 versus $12,400) *and* more left in their accounts ($15,000 versus $10,000).

Premature distributions: Employees who receive distributions from their 401(k) plan before they die, reach age $59\frac{1}{2}$, are disabled, or retire after reaching age 55 can expect to pay a 10 percent penalty in addition to ordinary income tax on the distribution amount.

Hardship distributions: Most 401(k) plans will not allow employee distributions from the plan unless the employee is terminated, becomes disabled, dies, or is separated from service. A hardship distribution may be the only way to take money out of your plan if you do not meet any of those criteria. For a distribution to qualify as a hardship distribution, it must satisfy two requirements:

◆ It must be due to the employee's immediate and heavy financial need.

◆ It must be necessary to satisfy that need.

Hardship distributions are subject to ordinary income tax and to the 10 percent IRS penalty for withdrawals before age 59½. The following are examples of immediate and heavy need:

◆ Medical expenses previously incurred by the employee, his or her spouse, or dependents; amounts necessary for any of these persons to obtain medical care

◆ Costs incurred in purchasing a principal residence (this does not include mortgage payments)

◆ Tuition and related educational expenses for the next year of post-secondary education for the employee, his or her spouse, or dependents

◆ Payments to prevent eviction from or foreclosure on a principal residence

$$ Note: Many plans that allow hardship distributions will not allow employee participation in the plan for one year following the distribution.

Summary

Before you know it, you are celebrating five years with the same company and wondering where the time went. How much could you have saved if you had been investing all that time in your retirement plan? Why put it off? It is easy to feel intimidated by the financial jargon and perplexing literature written to define your 401(k) or 403(b) plan. These items alone have deterred many people from taking that important first step to save something from each paycheck for later years. Having read this chapter, you should

have a better understanding of the advantages and disadvantages of 401(k) and 403(b) plans as well as definitions
for terms commonly used.

The following chapters will break down the complexi-
ties of saving for retirement and teach you how to be fiscally
fit. Take time *now* to think about retirement—today will soon
be yesterday.

Chapter Two

Your Plan Document

When you become eligible to join your 401(k) or 403(b) plan, you will receive a plan description. It will explain the composition of this voluntary, tax-qualified investment program created to help you save and invest for your future retirement. The document defines general terms, rules, and investment options of the plan. We recommend keeping all of your plan information and quarterly statements in a designated file that you can refer to in the future. In addition to the plan literature, your employee benefits counselor should be available when you have a question or problem with the information.

Questions and Answers Covered in Your Plan Document

What is the plan year?

Your plan year can be any specified 12-month duration, such as June 1 to May 31—not necessarily January 1 to December 31. Why is it important to know this? Your ability to borrow or withdraw funds may depend on how many full plan years you have contributed. Also, your employer's matching contribution may change from plan year to plan year, as may guaranteed rates on certain investment options. Be aware of the specific time frames in your plan so you don't miss making an important move or change.

How is the plan managed?

This section should name the trustee of the plan and your local administrator. Learning about the history and experience of your plan trustee and administrator can give you extra peace of mind. Within the plan, each investment option can have a separate manager, who may be different from the trustee and administrator. This information should be made available to you in individual prospectuses on the particular investment options.

When am I eligible to participate?

This section will detail your company's rules for participation. You may be eligible after you have completed one year of employment or after a certain number of hours. (Special rules may apply if you have a break in your employment service before you complete the requirement for participation.) This may be up to you to find out, so don't count on your employer to notify you when you are eligible.

How do I enroll?

Many plans will request that you fill out required paperwork at least one month prior to eligibility. It is important to ask for materials and get questions answered well ahead of time, so you do not delay the process. Time is money!

When do payroll deductions begin?

Your plan will define when deductions begin, such as the fifteenth day of the month after you enroll. At this time you should know how much will be deducted and when to prepare for a new bottom line on your paycheck.

How much can I contribute?

This will depend on the maximum and minimum percentage contributions allowed by your plan and on your salary or hourly wage. There may be different guidelines for hourly workers and salaried workers. Generally, base pay for hourly workers means pay for the average work week, excluding overtime. For salaried workers, base pay may or may not include overtime or bonuses. You can contribute any amount up to your plan limit and the legal limit ($9,240 in 1994). Federal tax law limits the total amount of personal and company contributions to the lesser of 25 percent of your taxable compensation or $30,000.

$$ Note: Due to IRS requirements, certain restrictions may be placed on the amounts and percentages that highly compensated employees can contribute.

401(k) Dilemma: Billy currently contributes 6 percent to his 401(k) account. He recently received a 4 percent raise and knew plenty of ways he could spend the extra cash. As the old saying goes, if you don't have it, you won't spend it, so he decided to split the raise with his 401(k) plan, increasing his contribution by 2 percent and spending the remaining 2 percent. If you aren't already contributing the maximum allowed by your plan, consider splitting each raise you receive—half to spend now and half to go into your retirement account until you reach the maximum.

How and when can I change my contribution?

This will vary from company to company, but can be monthly, quarterly or semi-annually. Under most circumstances, requests to change, suspend, or cease contributions must be filed with the plan administrator by a specified date in order to be effective for the next contribution. Keep in mind that if you stop contributing, the matching contributions (free money) from your employer will stop also.

What are the investment options in the plan?

This section should list all of the available investment options along with a complete description of each. You may also want to request an individual prospectus for each option to learn more about its holdings, manager, and previous total return. Each choice will have a different investment objective, a separate level of risk, and will produce distinct investment results, so it is important to read and understand your options completely before investing. This portion of the plan document should also describe the rules and time frames for transferring from one investment option to another.

What are the investment options' past returns?

The investment options' historic results should be available to you at the time of enrollment. This data will help you determine in which options you would like to invest. Once you start investing, you should receive a statement quarterly, which will update you on your investment performance. It will show you the amount you have invested in each option and the current market value of your account. Many 401(k) plans have a toll-free telephone number that allows daily access to account balances and information. This technology gives you the added incentive to stay current with your investment options, ask questions, and make changes as needed.

401(k) Tip: Make it a habit to call between statements for updated information and the performance of various investment options. Don't let quarterly or annual statements hand you an unpleasant surprise.

Will I incur any expenses for the plan?

There are certain costs to having a 401(k) plan, and not all employers pick up the whole tab. Investment management fees for individual fund management may be shared between you and your employer. Who pays for what should be clearly stated in your account literature. This includes brokerage fees, commissions, and all other expenses incurred by the trustee in buying or selling investments. While you may be responsible for some costs, they are normally less than you would assume outside your plan in a similar transaction. For example, the costs involved for you to buy or sell shares of stock in the open market is probably higher than the costs assumed by the fund manager, due to the quantities involved. While your transaction may be for 100 shares, the fund manager may be trading thousands of shares and receiving a substantial discount on commissions. (We will return to fees in Chapter 8.)

How are the company contributions invested?

Matching contributions may be given in cash, to invest as you choose within plan options, or they may come in the form of common stock of your company. If your company's stock is publicly traded, this may be a way for management to encourage employees to become shareholders. This section of the plan document will explain how and when shares are purchased, on what exchange the stock is traded, and where to find daily prices. If company contributions are not invested in company stock, how they are invested will be fully explained here.

What are the rules for distributions?

Rules for withdrawals and loans will differ from company to company but they generally will not allow withdrawls unless you retire, reach age 59½, are disabled, die, or leave the company.. While the plan is designed for the accumulation of retirement savings, extenuating circumstances may require use of the funds before that time. Generally, you must complete a written application in order to withdraw funds from your account. Your plan document will specify how long it will take to receive your funds and the date to be used for the valuation of your individual investments. You will be responsible for federal income tax on the amount withdrawn unless you are making a direct transfer or rollover to another custodian. You may also owe a 10 percent IRS penalty, depending on your age and the reason for the withdrawal.

Some companies will allow you to take a loan from your 401(k) account. The time period of the loan may vary depending on individual company policy. The interest rate charged will be stated in this section; it may be a fixed rate for the life of the loan, or variable, such as "prime rate plus one percentage point." Loan repayment is generally accomplished through payroll deduction unless you are no longer employed by the company. Your account balance will be used as collateral for your promissory note (a promise to pay) to your employer. In most cases no more than two loans can be outstanding at any time.

Who gets my money if I die?

If you are married, your spouse is automatically the beneficiary when you die unless he or she has agreed to another beneficiary in writing. If you are not married, you may designate one or more beneficiaries to receive the assets upon your death. Always have a beneficiary named in your plan.

A sample plan statement is provided in Table 2-1. While all statement formats are different, they share the same basic content and with practice you should have no trouble reading yours.

Summary

If you have any questions about your 401(k) plan, you should contact the plan administrator or benefits department of your company. This number should be listed within the plan's documents. Read this information carefully!

Table 2-1   Whitey and Sons Corporation

Savings Plan
Retirement Plan Account Statement
April 1, 1994–June 30, 1994

Rick Macdonald   Social Security Number 357-11-0000
519 N. Lincoln   Call R. Rowlings 1-800-555-1211
New York, NY 10021   Report any errors within 60 days

Beginning Balance	$18,763.27
Change This Period	$655.87
Ending Balance	$19,419.14

Investment	Beginning Balance	Ending Balance	Ending Shares
Guaranteed Inv. Contract	$7,505.31	$7,767.66	7,767.66
Growth & Income Fund	$11,257.96	$11,651.48	881.35
Total Balance	$18,763.27	$19,419.14	

Activity Summary	
Transaction	Amount
Beginning Balance	$18,763.27
Contribution	$359.28
Dividends and Growth	$296.59
Ending Balance	$19,419.14

Activity This Period						
	Beginning Balance	Contributions and Other Purchases	Withdrawals and Redemptions	Dividends	Gain/ Loss	Ending Balance
Company Match	$3,218.94	$46.87	$0.00	$20.31	$30.46	$3,316.58
Rollover	$3,776.44	$0.00	$0.00	$23.67	$35.51	$3,835.62
Salary Deferral	$11,767.89	$312.41	$0.00	$74.66	$111.98	$12,266.94
Total	$18,763.27	$359.28	$0.00	$118.64	$177.95	$19,419.14

Table 2-1   Whitey and Sons Corporation (cont'd)

Share Prices and Average Cost on June 30, 1994		
Investment	Price Per Share (6-30-94)	Average Cost
Guaranteed Inv Contract	$1.00	$1.00
Equity Income Fund	$17.11	
Growth and Income Fund	$13.22	$11.85
Balanced Fund	$14.05	
International Stock Fund	$11.07	

Investment Allocation on June 30,1994		
Investment	Price Per Share (6-30-94)	Average Cost
Guaranteed Inv. Contract	50.0%	50.0%
Equity Income Fund		
Growth and Income Fund	50.0%	50.0%
Balanced Fund		
International Stock Fund		
Total	100.0%	100.0%

Year-to-Date Account History			
Type of Money	Contributions	Dividends + Gain/Loss	Withdrawals
Company Match	$60.29	$99.90	$0.00
Rollover	$0.00	$116.87	$0.00
Salary Deferral	$401.86	$366.11	$0.00
Total YTD	$462.15	$582.88	$0.00

Inception-to-Date Account History			
Type of Money	Contributions	Dividends + Gain/Loss	Withdrawals
Company Match	$2,366.95	$1,043.63	$0.00
Rollover	$1,964.54	$2,058.08	$0.00
Salary Deferral	$9,361.50	$3,195.44	$0.00
Total	$13,692.99	$6,297.15	$0.00

Chapter Three

Piecing Together Your Investment Pyramid

After saving for years, your 401(k) plan could turn into your single biggest asset, potentially larger than the value of your home or any of your other investments. It is therefore easy to understand why it is critical to invest each and every dollar carefully. This chapter will help you put investment choices in their proper perspective. It isn't a complicated, technical process that only a financial wizard can unravel; in fact, with time and practice, it is a highly manageable procedure. We will use a step-by-step process to make choosing new options or analyzing old ones much easier.

401(k) Tip: When it comes to financial decisions, many people can tell you what to do *once*, but it is critical for you to know what to do, when to do it, and why you did it, all on a regular basis.

Three Steps to Financial Success

The hardest part is getting started. Begin by blocking off a few hours of quiet time to work with your financial resources. Take time to find out exactly where you are financially, think about where you want to go, and plan how you are going to get there. It takes time, but it's worth it. This process involves evaluating your personal financial situation and learning how to select good investments using the step-by-step sequence. We call this process the "Three Steps to Financial Success."

- ◆ *Step One:* Where you are—compiling a list of your investable funds and finding out exactly what you own.

- ◆ *Step Two:* Where you are going—deciding what your overall financial goals and needs are.

- ◆ *Step Three:* How to get there—a strategy to analyze the options of your 401(k) plan and other investments in order to reach those goals.

Step 1: Where you are

In Step One, you identify what you have by creating your own personal investment pyramid. To put together your personal pyramid you will first need to have a clear understanding of the basic investment pyramid. This is a commonly used visual aid that helps to categorize the relative risks and expected total return of many different investments. In each successive level, as you move from the bottom of the pyramid to the top, investments are characterized by more risk and a higher expected total return.

Examples of investments that fit in each level of the investment pyramid are shown in Figure 3-1. We will discuss the various levels of the pyramid along with each level's investment objectives, risks, and returns. Keep in mind as you read that this is a general format, which has been adapted for use by many professionals. If your plan

Figure 3-1   The Investment Pyramid

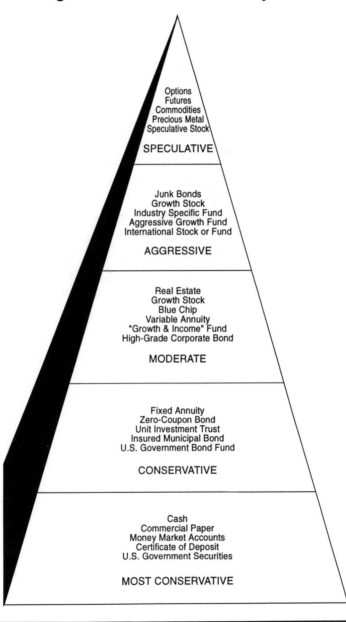

Options
Futures
Commodities
Precious Metal
Speculative Stock

SPECULATIVE

Junk Bonds
Growth Stock
Industry Specific Fund
Aggressive Growth Fund
International Stock or Fund

AGGRESSIVE

Real Estate
Growth Stock
Blue Chip
Variable Annuity
"Growth & Income" Fund
High-Grade Corporate Bond

MODERATE

Fixed Annuity
Zero-Coupon Bond
Unit Investment Trust
Insured Municipal Bond
U.S. Government Bond Fund

CONSERVATIVE

Cash
Commercial Paper
Money Market Accounts
Certificate of Deposit
U.S. Government Securities

MOST CONSERVATIVE

educator or financial adviser uses a slightly different pyramid, try to combine its content with the pyramid you see here, rather than throwing either one out.

The investment pyramid

Level 1: Most conservative
Investment objective: income and preservation of principal
These investments are designed for income and preservation of principal. They are short-term, with high liquidity and low total return. Examples are cash, money market accounts, certificates of deposit (CDs), and U.S. government securities. Your emergency reserves should be invested at this level and should equal three to six months' living expenses (not income). Your total return will be interest, not price appreciation. We recommend that you never have more than 15 percent percent of your investable funds in this level.

$$ *Note:* If emergency reserves exceed 15 percent of your investable funds, this is an acceptable deviation from the guideline.

Level 2: Conservative
Investment objective: income
These investments carry a little more risk and promise a little more total return. Like the investments in Level 1, they are designed primarily for income and preservation of principal. Examples are U.S. government zero-coupon bonds, insured municipal bonds, unit investment trusts (UITs), fixed annuities, and some U.S. government bond mutual funds. Total return of the investments in this level will be mostly interest, but there may be some fluctuation in principal value.

Level 3: Moderate

Investment objective: growth and income

These investments are designed for growth, and total return is expected to come from moderate change in principal with modest income. Because these investments are growth-oriented, their prices will fluctuate more and they may be less liquid than investments in the bottom two levels. For this reason, your outlook should be long-term (three to five years) for any investment in the moderate level.

Examples of investments are high-grade corporate bonds, variable annuities, mutual funds in the "growth and income" category, some stocks (such as blue chip stocks), and possibly investment real estate (other than your home).

Level 4: Aggressive

Investment objective: aggressive growth

These investments are designed for long-term growth in principal and higher total return. A change in principal value is the primary component of total return in this level. Common stocks may provide little or no dividend income and will carry significant risk along with their equally significant projected return. They may be very volatile and/or have very low liquidity. Examples of aggressive investments are low-grade corporate bonds (also known as "junk" bonds), some growth stocks, industry specific mutual funds (funds that invest in the stock of companies in a particular industry, such as oil, health care, etc.), mutual funds labeled "aggressive growth," and international stocks, bonds, and mutual funds.

Level 5: Speculative

Investment objective: Speculation

You can invest in the speculative level only with money you can afford to lose. If you win, it's great; if you lose, it won't change your life. These investments are very risky; and though they make exciting stories, the losers far outnumber the winners. Total return in this level comes from price change (which can go to zero as quickly as it can double), rarely from income. Examples are futures, options, commodities, precious metals, speculative stocks, and penny stocks (stocks whose price is less than $5).

Never have more than 5 percent of your investable funds invested in the Speculative level.

401(k) Tip: If you invest in the speculative level, try this strategy. Set a limit on the amount you are willing to lose, much like you might on a trip to a casino. Invest that amount. *If you win,* cash out, take your profits, and invest them at a less risky level of the pyramid. Reinvest your original principal in another speculative investment. *If you lose,* don't buy any more speculative investments this year. Next year, decide if you want to try investing in the speculative level again, but do it only with money you can afford to lose.

Your personal investment pyramid

No matter how much or how little money you have, everyone has a personal pyramid. To find out what yours looks like, you must compile all of your financial records and look at the whole picture. Only your "investable funds" belong in your personal investment pyramid. They are all of your assets *except* your primary residence and any art, jewelry, or collectibles, unless you have purchased them with the idea of selling later for a profit. (If you wouldn't sell it for cash to invest, don't include it in your investable funds.) We include the money you put aside for emergencies, savings, checking, CDs, retirement (401(k)/403(b)), stocks, bonds, mutual funds, the cash value of life insurance policies, *everything* you own to generate income or growth. Each of your investments can be categorized in one of the five levels of the investment pyramid and the end result will be your own personal portfolio in the shape of a pyramid.

How is this done?

◆ List everything you own on the appropriate level of the blank pyramid in Figure 3-2, approximating each item's current market value.

◆ Calculate the total of what you own in each individual level.

◆ Calculate the total of all levels combined.

◆ Calculate the percentage of your total investable funds that are in each level by dividing each level's total by the pyramid total.

401(k) Tip: Complete and analyze your personal pyramid on an annual basis so that when planning each year or making an important financial decision you can begin with "Where you are." This snapshot of your financial condition is an annual report card, showing your progress.

Figure 3-2   Your Personal Pyramid

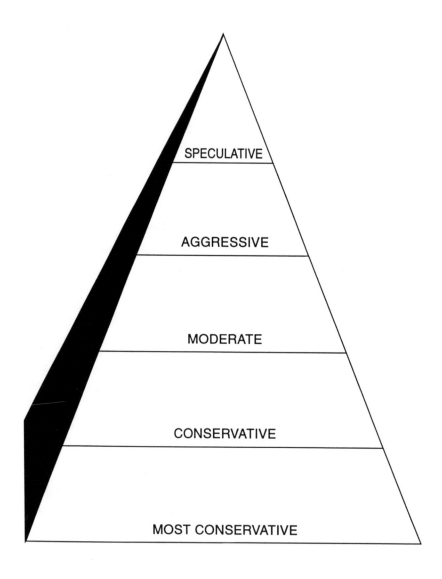

Completing your pyramid may take several hours and, like many endeavors, the first time is the hardest. It is impossible to keep current with today's complex market, but if you have this framework and know where you are, you can make better decisions. Two of the most common problems with money are not knowing what you have and not making your money work for you. With the annual analysis of your personal pyramid, you will always know exactly what you have and where you are.

$$ Note: While this book concentrates on the money you are investing in your 401(k) or 403(b) plan, your personal pyramid deals with *all* your investable funds, showing how your retirement savings fit into the big picture.

Step 2: Where you are going

The second step to financial success is to determine where you are going. This involves determining which of the four financial stages (not ages) of life you are in and what percentage of your money should be invested at each level of your personal investment pyramid based on your stage. The recommended percentages are your investment goals, or where you are going.

401(k) Dilemma: Mark said to us, "I am 40 years old; this is how much money I have, how should it be invested?" Without knowing more about him, we couldn't offer any suggestions. Why? Because people have different financial situations and needs, even at the same age. At 40, he might have children who are 18 and 20 years old or children who are 2 and 4. Or he might not have any. His goal might be to retire in five years at 45, or in 25 years, at age 65. Your personal circumstances

and goals, not your age, determine your stage of life
and, in turn, how your money should be invested.

The Four Financial Stages of Life

Take the next five minutes to decide which financial stage
you are in right now. Some guidelines follow:

Getting Started

The first financial stage of life is "Getting Started." This
includes your first job or establishing a career; determining your budget for living and saving expenses; buying
furniture and cars; saving for a home; and, most impor-
tantly, establishing an emergency fund of three to six
months' living expenses in a highly liquid investment,
such as a money market.

In this beginning stage you are constructing a strong
financial base. Generally, you will not have much extra
cash after paying living expenses, but it is imperative to
start your financial future by *earning some interest*, even if
you must pay some interest to others. Save what you can,
and watch it grow. Your investment outlook for this first
stage of life is long term.

Getting Growing

In the second stage, "Getting Growing," you begin to
make more money and to spend more on large items, such
as your first home. This stage may include getting married
and having children and saving for their education; dual
incomes may be necessary to support growing families.

Even with the high cost of living in this stage, you should begin investing actively for retirement. Small amounts grow large over time with the power of compounding, so your investment outlook again is long term.

Getting Comfortable

The third financial stage of life is "Getting Comfortable." This stage begins after major responsibilities and high living expenses are over. If there were children, they have left the nest and no longer need your support. Now is the time to invest larger amounts of money for retirement, making sure your dollars are growing effectively to provide adequate support when you need it. Since you still may be years away from retirement, your investment outlook is long term, but you take less risk because you have less time to make up lost principal. However, you should continue to own some moderate- and aggressive-level growth investments to protect yourself against inflation.

Some families will skip the "Getting Comfortable" stage. For those of us who marry and/or have children later in life, we may move from "Getting Growing" right into "Taking it Easy" as children leave the nest at the onset of retirement. If you think this will happen to you, begin to save more for retirement while you are in the earlier stages.

401(k) Tip: Having a family when you are older and more financially secure makes sense, but don't spend all the money on college educations while neglecting to invest in your retirement fund.

Taking It Easy

In the fourth financial stage of life, "Taking It Easy," retirement begins. You may be 50 or you may be 70. Whatever your age, this could be the longest stage of your life.

$$ Money Mistake: The biggest mistake people make in the "Taking It Easy" stage is saying, "I don't need to manage my money; I'm retired." WRONG! WRONG! WRONG! If you don't earn an income, that money you aren't managing is all you have.

Similar to the "Getting Comfortable" stage, you will need a percentage of growth investments during retirement to protect you from inflation. A hamburger doesn't cost what it did 30 years ago; what do you think it will cost in 2020? The growth portion of your personal pyramid protects your buying power.

401(k) Tip: Saving for retirement isn't accumulating dollars, it's accumulating buying power to support a desired standard of living.

Figure 3-3 depicts goal pyramids and percentage guidelines for each of the four financial stages of life.

Step 3: How to get there: Comparing pyramids

Once you have created your personal pyramid, compare it with the goal pyramid for your financial stage of life. See anything wrong? The two pyramids are probably not the

Figure 3-3   Personal Pyramid Goals for the Four Financial Stages of Life

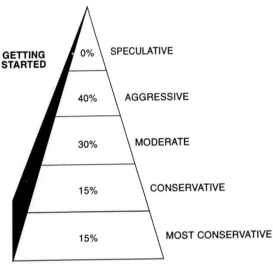

GETTING
STARTED

0% SPECULATIVE

40% AGGRESSIVE

30% MODERATE

15% CONSERVATIVE

15% MOST CONSERVATIVE

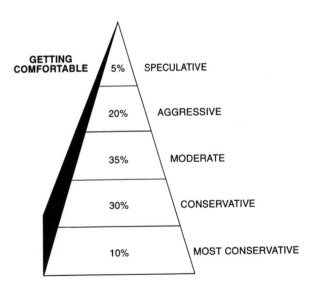

GETTING
COMFORTABLE

5% SPECULATIVE

20% AGGRESSIVE

35% MODERATE

30% CONSERVATIVE

10% MOST CONSERVATIVE

©*MONEYWISE*, 1992.

Figure 3-3   Personal Pyramid Goals
for the Four Financial Stages of Life (cont'd)

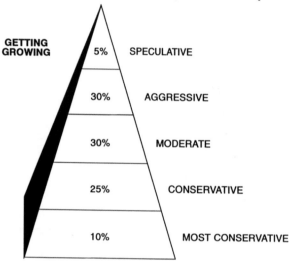

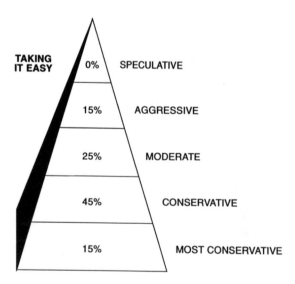

©*MONEYWISE*, 1992.

same. Don't worry. Step 3, how to get there, allows you to make the changes necessary to bring your personal pyramid closer to your goal pyramid. By comparing percentages in each level of your personal pyramid to your goals, you can see which levels need more of your total funds and which levels need less. Anything within 5 percent of the recommended percentage is acceptable.

Let's take the Young's personal pyramid in Figure 3-4 as an example. They have listed all their investable funds and allocated each item to its proper level on the pyramid. They have subtotaled each level, and divided each of those numbers by the pyramid total to find the percentage listed on each level. This is their Personal Pyramid; this is where they are.

Figure 3-4   Young's Personal Pyramid

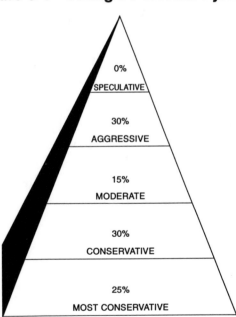

Next, they will take Step 2. Their children are in high school and they are beginning to think about retirement. The Youngs are in the "Getting Growing" stage of life, and their goal pyramid now looks like the middle pyramid depicted in Figure 3-5).

In Step 3, they have compared the pyramids (see Figure 3-5) to see what they should change.

The speculative level is fine at 0 percent compared with a goal of 0–5 percent.

The aggressive level goal is 30 percent and they have 30 percent; again, no change is necessary here.

Their moderate level is 15 percent of their pyramid total and the goal is 30 percent; we'll mark a plus (+) next to that level because it is below the guideline.

The conservative level is 30 percent versus a goal of 25 percent; that one gets an o.k., because it is within 5 percent of the guideline.

The most conservative level is overconcentrated at 25 percent because the goal is only 10 percent; a minus (–) goes next to that level.

Now the Youngs know just what to do the next time they are faced with an important financial decision. If they are adding to their investable funds due to a bonus, or maybe just more in monthly savings, where should they invest? That's right, they should invest in the moderate level.

Figure 3-5 Three Steps to Financial Success

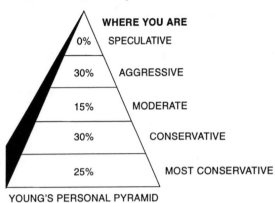

WHERE YOU ARE

0%	SPECULATIVE
30%	AGGRESSIVE
15%	MODERATE
30%	CONSERVATIVE
25%	MOST CONSERVATIVE

YOUNG'S PERSONAL PYRAMID

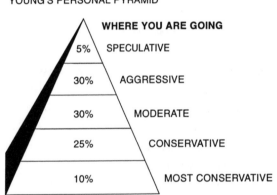

WHERE YOU ARE GOING

5%	SPECULATIVE
30%	AGGRESSIVE
30%	MODERATE
25%	CONSERVATIVE
10%	MOST CONSERVATIVE

GETTING GROWING GOAL PYRAMID %

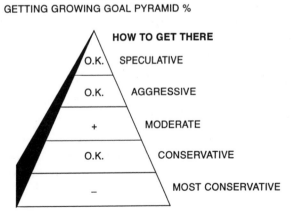

HOW TO GET THERE

O.K.	SPECULATIVE
O.K.	AGGRESSIVE
+	MODERATE
O.K.	CONSERVATIVE
–	MOST CONSERVATIVE

401(k) Dilemma: If the Youngs have CDs or U.S. Government bonds maturing in the most conservative level, should they reinvest in the same level?

Probably not, since they need to decrease their concentration in the most conservative level. They should take these proceeds and reinvest them where they need more—in this case, the moderate level.

Figure 3-6 is a worksheet of the three steps for you to complete.

Summary

You should now understand why it is wise to compare your personal pyramid to your goal pyramid every time you make an investment decision (and at least annually) to monitor your progress. Your individual investments can change, your financial stage of life may change, and investing habits and opportunities can change, not to mention interest rates, the stock market, and the economy.

You may have noticed how the percentages changed through the four stages of life. In the first stage, you should have 70 percent in the top three (growth) levels of the pyramid and 30 percent in the bottom two (income). As you reach the "Taking It Easy" stage, your percentages shift to 60 percent in the bottom two levels and 40 percent in the top three. The key is to give your personal pyramid proper attention throughout your life, set goals, and follow percentage guidelines. In retirement, you should not have to worry how you spend your money, but enjoy how you spend your time.

Figure 3-6   Three Steps to Financial Success

Figure 3-6   Three Steps to Financial Success
(continued)

**Figure 3-6   Three Steps to Financial Success
(continued)**

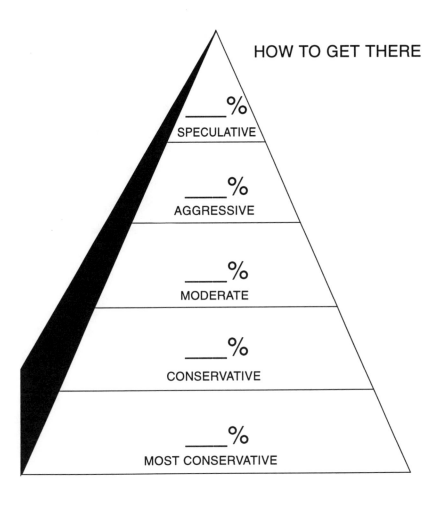

Chapter Four

Your Plan Options— Where's the Risk?

Stock funds, bond funds, company stock, and money markets ... which one or which combination is right for you? You'll probably never get it perfect, but after some examples and analysis, you should be able to get close. John Templeton, the famous mutual fund manager, says when it comes to choosing investments, his goal is to be right two out of every three times. We all make mistakes, but doing nothing is the biggest mistake you can make. Here are some other common ones:

$$ Money Mistakes:
1) Investing too conservatively in investments without growth potential.
2) Trying to be a market-timer (buying and selling frequently on short-term market news).
3) Not diversifying among investment options.
4) Investing with a short-term rather than long-term outlook.
5) Investing without sufficient knowledge and financial education (never invest in something you don't understand).

Deciding how to invest your 401(k) contributions can be difficult, but don't agonize over it. What is important is to make educated, well-reasoned financial decisions. Typically, you will be offered between four and six investment options in your plan and once you completely understand how they work, you'll be able to make the most of your money. Sure, it is much easier to simply ask a co-worker what investment options to choose, rather than digging in and doing the research for yourself. Just remember everyone has different needs and objectives, so investments that are good for a co-worker may not be right for you. You wouldn't count on someone else to take care of you in retirement, so don't count on them to make investment decisions that will.

401(k) Tip: No one will watch your money like you will.

Begin by taking a few hours to use the three steps to financial success outlined in Chapter 3. This will give you a direction for making individual investment choices. Only then are you ready to look at the options within your plan and start choosing how to allocate the money.

Before you analyze each option, you will need to learn more about the relationship between risk and reward. You may love to bungee jump, drive race cars, play blackjack, and shoot whitewater river rapids, or you may be the quiet type looking for nothing but peace and tranquility out of your daily life. In either case, you should be aware of the risks that you face when you invest. Determining your attitude about risk and deciding which type of reward best matches your retirement goals will help you follow through with a financial strategy. You don't have to be a high-roller to take risks; all investments, even cash, have some risk. No matter what the investment, it is useful to learn what can go wrong and how to manage the possibilities.

401(k) Tip: The greater the expected return, the greater the investment risk. If you think of just one thing each time you consider an investment, think of this.

Five Types of Risk

In this section we will define five types of investment risk. As you analyze your own investments, you will be able to identify and balance each type of risk in addition to balancing your goal pyramid levels.

Inflation risk

You experience this every day with anything you purchase. Will a dollar's worth of goods today be worth a dollar five years from now or, for an investment, will the dollars returned from an investment be worth less than the dollars invested? For example, if you earn 4 percent on your investments, but lose 5 percent of their value to inflation, you have less purchasing power at the end of a year than when you started.

In the last 20 years, the rate of inflation has averaged about 6 percent. At the same rate, $1.00 will only be worth $0.31 twenty years from now. In real purchasing power terms, how many loaves of bread can you buy today with $1? Maybe one, if you use a coupon. However, $1 bought around three loaves in 1970, six in 1950 and ten in 1940. The point is that you face inflation risk with any investment that pays back a fixed dollar amount in the future, with no chance of growth in principal. This includes CDs, bonds, money market accounts, and fixed annuities. In contrast, hard assets, such as real estate, collectibles, and precious metals, often rise in value with inflation. Investments such as stocks have the potential for growth, which can offset the loss in purchasing power of the dollar.

Interest rate risk

There is one thing you can bank on when it comes to interest rates: they rarely stay the same from year to year. As they fluctuate, their movements will affect the value of your investments. Interest rate risk generally applies to fixed-income investments such as bonds or CDs and can be divided into two categories: *value and reinvestment rate risk.*

a) **Value risk:** When interest rates rise, bond prices usually fall and vice versa. Thus, if you own a bond and market interest rates rise, the market value (what you could sell it for) goes down. Why? Let's say you have a bond that pays 7 percent interest, and after one year new bonds are paying 8 percent interest. Is your bond as valuable as one that pays a higher rate? Certainly not. A buyer would not be willing to pay as much for a bond with a lower-than-average rate. If market rates had gone down, your bond would have increased in value. If you own individual bonds and their market price goes down, it doesn't mean you need to sell. If you bought them for fixed income and you still expect to receive the full face value at maturity, you will not lose money by holding them. The risk lies in the event that you need to sell before maturity, in which case you would receive a lower price than you paid.

Bond funds are especially vulnerable to value interest rate risk, because they have no maturity date. An ordinary bond, which has lost value due to rising interest rates, can be held until maturity, and you'll receive the full face value—you do not lose money. However, because bond funds do not have a maturity date, there is no promise of receiving the full value at maturity. Mutual funds are priced at current market value of the securities held in the fund, which may mean the depressed market price of the individual bonds held in the fund.

b) Reinvestment rate risk: This is the risk that if interest rates fall after you make an investment, you will be reinvesting the interest payments that you receive at a lower rate. It also means that when the investment matures, or if it is called before maturity, your choices of reinvesting the principal could result in your earning a lower rate of interest.

401(k) Tip: Callable bonds are especially vulnerable to reinvestment rate risk, because the issuer has the right to call the bonds or pay them off before maturity. The issuer will naturally do this when interest rates fall because they can issue new bonds and pay a lower rate, just as you do when refinancing your home. When the bondholders get their investments back unexpectedly, they face a lower rate of return for reinvestment.

Business risk

Business risk is encountered in investments such as common stocks and corporate bonds. This is the risk, which faces an individual corporation, from such diverse sources as management errors, faulty products, poor financial planning, marketing mistakes, and so on. If the numbers on the balance sheet or income statement start to get in the "red," your investments may be in trouble; the most extreme result of business risk is bankruptcy. If you hold common stock, you are at the bottom of the list behind lawyers, the IRS, banks, bondholders, and preferred stockholders when it comes to getting any money back.

The best way to avoid business risk is by practicing the principle of *diversification*. When you own stocks of individual companies, collect 15 or more different stocks individually or through mutual funds. Experts say that the business risk of any one company is effectively diversified away when you have the cushion of 14 others.

Market risk

The type of risk that remains in a diversified portfolio is market risk (also known as economic risk), the risk that financial markets, or the economy as a whole, performs poorly, thus causing investments to change in value regardless of the fundamentals of individual investments. The stock market crash of 1987 is an example of stock market risk. The economic downturn of the early 1990s is an example of market or economic risk for real estate investments. These risks cannot be controlled by the investor but will affect virtually all investments. Figure 4-1 depicts business and market risk.

Liquidity risk

This is the risk that you cannot sell an investment quickly without losing principal. The appraised value of your home or your collection of Chinese porcelain can't put

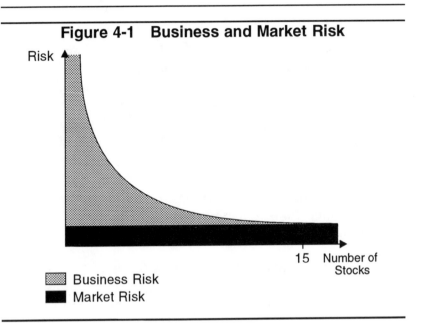

Figure 4-1   Business and Market Risk

Business Risk
Market Risk

cash in your pocket if you cannot find a buyer. Liquidity risk affects investments that do not have active secondary markets and investments that are in very volatile or cyclical markets, such as real estate.

***401(k)* Dilemma:** Patty and Dan have $100,000 of investable funds. They have the following investments:
  $25,000 in a money market account
  $10,000 in U.S. saving bonds
  $15,000 in growth stock mutual funds
  $50,000 in Dan's company stock
What risks do they face?

401(k) Solution: They have 35 percent of their portfolio in fixed income investments (bonds and money market), which are subject to inflation risk, and 65 percent (stock

funds and company stock) in investments that are subject to market risk. Business risk from the 50 percent in
company stock is their most dangerous risk. Dan is
counting on a paycheck from this company as well as for
one-half of the value of their investments. If the company
had problems and he were fired without notice, they
would lose an income while at the same time their investment in the company stock could be losing value.
Unless the investment is in profit-sharing or a company
401(k) matching program in which they have no choice,
they should diversify this holding.

Don't be an armchair quarterback—get involved! The
danger in investment risk is the unknown. Being aware of
the risks you face can help you to diversify the risk you
take.

Sample Investment Options

All retirement plans are different, so we'll offer a few sample investment options, some of which you may find in
your plan. We will highlight where each fits in the investment pyramid, along with its advantages and disadvantages.

Fund A: Money market fund

This is a pool of investments that yields current short-term
interest rates by investing in short-term debt securities,
such as U.S. Treasury bills. It seeks to maintain a consistent value of $1 per share. Money market funds are often
called cash equivalents because of their stability.

Pyramid level: Most Conservative

Advantages: Safety—there is little or no chance of losing principal.

Disadvantages/risk: While this is a safe investment in terms of stability of principal, the rate of inflation can exceed your earnings, making it possible to lose purchasing power.

Your objective: Use it only as a short-term shelter because it cannot provide growth.

Fund B: Fixed-income fund

This fund may include bonds, mortgages, preferred stocks, investment contracts with insurance companies (GICs), and/or other fixed-income securities such as U.S. Treasury bonds, Treasury bills, certificates of deposit, or money market accounts.

Pyramid level: Conservative

Advantages: Relative safety with low fluctuation of principal.

Disadvantages/risk: While fixed-income funds are generally considered to be very safe, they can lose principal quickly if market interest rates rise (interest rate risk). They also suffer from inflation risk.

Your objective: To obtain diversification when other funds are exposed to stock market fluctuations or to assume more principal stability as you reach retirement age.

Fund C: Guaranteed investment contracts (GICs)

A GIC is one of the most common fixed-rate investment options offered by 401(k) plans. Investors get a fixed yield for one to five years and the promise that they will not lose principal. Sounds good, *but* the "guarantee" behind a GIC is only as good as the insurance company issuing the contract. (See more about GICs in Chapter 8.)

Pyramid level: Conservative.

Advantages: Safety and preservation of principal.

Disadvantages/risk: The possibility that the issuing insurance company could become insolvent (business risk). If you are locked into long-term contracts, you could also miss out on higher returns in a period of rising interest rates.

Your objective: Short-term fixed income and relative safety.

Fund D: Balanced fund

A balanced fund provides a compromise between investing in stocks and bonds by investing in both. A balanced fund generally tries to maintain a mixture of large and small company stocks and long- and short-term bonds. The rationale is that stock and bond markets are different, often rising and falling at different times. The management style is designed to take advantage of the growth potential of stocks while limiting risk with income from bonds.

Pyramid level: Conservative to Moderate depending on the mix of stocks and bonds.

Advantages: Diversification, with the average total return being leveraged to the upside by the growth potential of the stocks and the downside being tempered by stability of interest income from various bonds.

Disadvantages/risk: Your principal value may fluctuate due to changes in the stocks held in the portfolio, resulting from general malaise in the stock market (market risk) or poor stock choices by the fund manager (business risk). It may also fluctuate due to changes in the value of the bonds held in the portfolio, most often caused by movements in market interest rates (interest rate risk). Generally, the stock and bond markets move independently, lowering your risk in a portfolio that holds both stocks and bonds. However, in some cases, the markets may move together. For example, an increase in interest rates will cause bond prices to fall and may forecast falling stock prices, if inflation fears are aroused.

Your objective: A long-term outlook with a balance of safety and growth.

Fund E: Indexed equity fund

This fund is designed to mirror the performance of a common stock index, usually the Standard & Poor's 500 Index (S&P 500), an index of 500 common stocks. When you hear that "the market" did well today, usually people are referring to either the S&P 500 Index or the Dow Jones Industrial Average (DJIA), an index of 30 blue-chip stocks. Over time, the stock market has outperformed all other investments. For example, in the last 20 years, the S&P 500 has an average annualized return of 11.7 percent every year. In other words, $1,000 invested in 1972 in a mutual fund indexed to the S&P 500 would have been worth $9,158 in

1992. The same $1,000, invested in 1972 in a fixed account composed of U.S. Treasury bonds, was worth only $3,207 in 1992. Many people pass up this investment option because they feel the stock market is too "risky." Keep in mind that even the apparent safety of cash or money market accounts can have hidden risks, such as inflation.

Pyramid level: Moderate

Advantages: Growth of principal and a higher average historic total return.

Disadvantages/risk: The fluctuation in principal due to movements in stock market (market risk). There are no guarantees that principal will increase in value.

Your objective: Long-term growth of principal through capital appreciation.

Fund F: Company stock fund

Many 401(k) plans in large companies whose common stock is publicly traded offer the employer's stock as one of the plan investment options. Employers often encourage investment in this fund, feeling that employees who are owners of the company will work harder and take an active interest in the bottom line. Many employees like it for similar reasons. Beyond receiving a paycheck, their jobs become a means to build the company and profit through an increased stock price.

Pyramid level: Moderate, Aggressive, or Speculative depending on the financial stability of the company. (See "Your Company Stock" in Chapter 5 for more information about analyzing your stock's investment potential.)

Advantages: The potential to increase the value of your investment as your company grows. As an integral part of your firm, you should have a genuine feel for how the stock should perform. You hear about your company's strengths and at the same time understand its weaknesses. You know how the business works and what could make or break long-range plans. This is a true advantage because many people buy stock and never know more than the company's stock symbol. Being both an employee and shareholder definitely gives you an inside edge.

Disadvantages/risk: Counting on a paycheck from, as well as investing in, your company means you are putting a lot of your eggs in one basket. If your company should have financial difficulties, you could find yourself without a job (or faced with salary freezes) at the same time your retirement savings in company stock are losing value due to falling prices. Also, because you own all of the same issue, you are facing a higher risk of price fluctuation and loss of principal than in a mutual fund with many different types of stocks whose prices fluctuate independently of one another. A company stock fund is most obviously subject to business risk, but is also affected by market and possibly liquidity risk, if the stock is not actively traded.

Your objective: To take advantage of what you believe is excellent growth potential. Furthermore, having employees as shareholders may help to shield the company from unwanted takeovers or other adversity. For every share you own, you have a say in the company's future.

$$ Note: It's fine to have some of your 401(k) money invested in company stock, however, don't bet the farm on one horse. The company stock fund may be a great place for a *portion* of your retirement savings.

Fund G: Aggressive fund

Different aggressive funds may be made up of small-company stocks, environmentally specific companies, or possibly international stocks. They are designed to provide high investor returns through rapid growth.

Pyramid level: Aggressive

Advantages: You expect a higher return of your dollars invested by assuming aggressive risk.

Disadvantages/risk: The price you pay for high potential return is high risk. These funds may fluctuate widely in value due to the business risk of small, new companies, the risk of stocks concentrated in one industry, or the different risks of international trade. International funds face the risk of currency fluctuation as well as company-specific (business), market, and liquidity risks. Do not invest here if your time horizon is fewer than five years, due to the potentially high volatility of these investments.

Objective: A long-term outlook with maximum growth in principal.

Your Plan Pyramid

How do all these funds fit in the basic investment pyramid? Now that we know more about each, let's match their investment objectives with the proper level of the pyramid to determine where they belong:

Level 5: Speculative   Fund F*
Level 4: Aggressive   Fund F* and G
Level 3: Moderate   Fund E and F*

Level 2: Conservative   Fund B, C, and D
Level 1: Most Conservative   Fund A

* The company stock fund could be in the moderate, aggressive, or speculative level of the pyramid depending on its financial stability and current condition.

See Figure 4-2 for a sample plan pyramid.

Figure 4-2 Sample Plan Pyramid

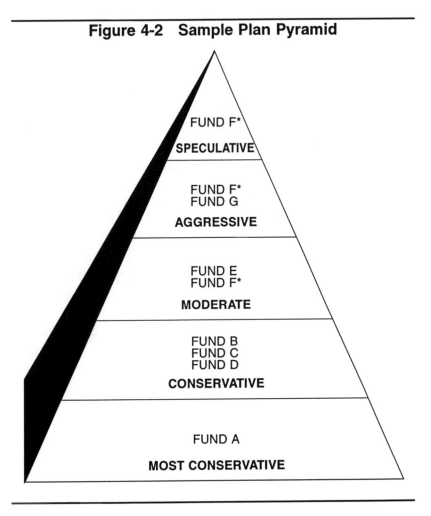

Summary

Knowing the risks you face when investing and learning more about your plan's options will help you make decisions that can maximize your investment returns while minimizing your risk.

In 1993, an aggregate of all 401(k) plans showed investments distributed in the following manner:

Guaranteed accounts	31%
Company stock	24%
Balanced accounts	13%
Equity accounts	11%
Money market accounts	9%
Bond accounts	5%
Miscellaneous accounts	7%

In 2003, overall 401(k) plan distribution averages are predicted to be substantially reduced in the guaranteed accounts (GICs) portion, about the same in company stock, but significantly increased in stock and bond accounts. This speculation is attributed to more involvement and understanding by 401(k) participants due to company-sponsored financial education programs. Also expected is higher participation due to greater understanding of investment options through in-depth analysis. The next chapter is devoted specifically to that subject.

Chapter Five

Analyzing Your Investment Options

Your plan may offer a wide array of investment choices, including some that sound very familiar and some you have never heard of. How can you choose between two mutual funds with comparable descriptions or among several in the same level of the investment pyramid? How do you know whether your company stock is a good buy or if you should avoid it right now? What do you need to know about annuity choices to make a good decision?

This section will help you with all of these dilemmas. It will discuss and explain the three most common types of investment options: mutual funds, stocks, and annuities. You will find questions to ask when investigating each investment option, a worksheet to help you compare different choices, and sources of objective rating information. While our discussion will pertain to your 401(k) or 403(b) plan options, this information can be used to make investment decisions outside your plan as well.

Mutual Funds

What is a mutual fund? A mutual fund is an investment company that makes investments on behalf of individuals and institutions. Each fund can be a combination of stocks, bonds, or other securities that are managed by professionals, providing investors a simple, convenient, and some-times less expensive method of investing.

The mutual fund pools money from many different investors who have similar objectives. A professional money manager makes investment decisions designed to meet the stated objectives of the fund. Each share of the fund represents ownership in all of the fund's underlying securi-ties, so shareholders who invest a few hundred dollars receive the same investment return per dollar as sharehold-ers who invest hundreds of thousands.

Mutual fund advantages

Diversification: Owning many different securities, which limits the risk of any one of them, is one of the biggest advantages to investing in mutual funds.

Professional management: Professional money manage-ment has long been available to institutions and wealthy investors. A mutual fund allows you access to expert man-agement no matter what amount you have invested.

Flexible investing: You are able to invest any amount above the minimum requirement (some funds have no minimum) and move with ease between other choices within the fund family.

Automatic reinvestment: You may automatically pur-chase more shares of the fund with dividends or capital gains that are earned.

When you are comparing mutual fund choices, whether they are privately managed by your 401(k) ad-ministrator or are well-known, publicly offered fund fami-lies such as Twentieth Century or Vanguard, there are several questions you can ask to be sure that you make an informed decision.

1) What is the fund's investment objective?

Your 401(k) plan's fund objectives may or may not correspond to the seven sample investment objectives explained in Chapter 4. However, if you look closely, you will probably find that your plan includes some variations on these main categories.

An important aspect of comparing funds to one another is that you compare apples to apples in terms of their risk level. Each fund's investment objective is the main determinant in deciding at which level of the investment pyramid it belongs. Remember the basis for the investment pyramid: as you move from the bottom to the top, both your expected return and your risk increase.

$$ Money Mistake: Larry's plan offered four funds, with average annual returns of 4.2 percent, 6.7 percent, 9.8 percent, and 14.3 percent. Larry didn't have any trouble deciding which fund to choose—he wanted the one with the highest return!

What was his mistake? Not looking at each investment objective as part of his decision-making process. Just three years from retirement, Larry took a big chance by choosing the riskiest fund offered.

Before you begin comparing rates of return, make sure that the investment objectives of the funds in question put them in the same level (i.e., risk level) of the investment pyramid. For example, a *small-company stock fund* and an *international stock fund* both belong in the aggressive level of the investment pyramid. If you have determined that you need to invest in this level, move on to the next question, knowing that their risk is comparable.

2) How well has the fund performed in the past?

If you don't have a crystal ball handy, you'll have to use past performance to anticipate what a fund could do in the future. While this isn't a foolproof method, past perform-ance is the best predictor we have and can be a good way to compare two different funds.

A phrase you will see often is *average annual return*. This generally means *total return* (dividends or interest + capital gain or loss) and is a calculated average of the time period in question.

Total return is an important theory because it tells you not only what you have earned from an investment (cur-rent return), but how much your original principal is worth (capital gain or loss). The sum of these two items is total return.

$$
\begin{matrix}
\text{Interest or} \\
\text{dividends} \\
\text{received}
\end{matrix}
+
\begin{matrix}
\text{Gain or loss} \\
\text{of principal in} \\
\text{original investment}
\end{matrix}
=
\begin{matrix}
\text{Total} \\
\text{Return}
\end{matrix}
$$

Think of the total return of an investment as you would the life of a tulip bulb. It yields blooms every spring throughout its lifetime. It may remain as a single bulb, or it may multiply, providing many more. The bulb is like the principal of an investment, remaining constant or increas-ing in size and number (or occasionally dying). Its blooms are like dividends, which occur at regular intervals throughout its lifetime. The total return from the tulip bulb is the sum of its yield in blooms and its remaining bulb or bulbs.

The five-year average annual total return is computed by taking the fund's beginning value and its value after five years, then calculating what annual rate of return that, five years in a row would have produced the ending value. While the individual years' rates of total return may fluctuate, making them difficult to compare, the average annual return can give you a good idea of long-term performance.

When comparing funds, concentrate on the following time frames:

◆ 1-year total return

◆ 3-year total return

◆ 5-year total return

◆ 10-year total return

401(k) Tip: Disregard returns for periods of less than one year, due to their temporary nature. Even the one-year return figure is less valuable than the others. Why? Because it is easy to be lucky with a few good picks that really boost performance *once*, but to have consistently good returns over three, five, or 10 years is more difficult—and requires a lot more than luck.

There are three ways to use total return figures:

1) *When you need help in deciding on a pyramid level.*

When you have a fund that doesn't fit into a category easily, check its average annual total returns. For example, in what level of the pyramid would you place a *high-yield bond fund*? You might be tempted to say, "Conservative," which is where most U.S. government bond funds belong. But, if the high-yield bond fund has total returns that are 3 percent to 5 percent higher than ordinary bond funds, you can assume that the fund is taking additional risk in order to earn that "high yield." Depending on how *much* higher the returns are, it might belong in either the moderate or aggressive level.

In another application, it is often difficult to decide whether a growth fund is moderate or aggressive. One hint is to check the volatility of its year-to-year annual returns. Given two funds with similar five- or 10-year total returns, the fund whose individual annual total returns fluctuate more widely is the more risky fund. High year-to-year volatility, especially with periodic negative annual total returns, indicates an aggressive-level fund.

2) *When you are comparing several funds in the same risk level.*

If your plan offers a large assortment of different funds or offers funds from several different families, you may have more than one fund to choose from in each level of the pyramid. If you have decided to invest in the moderate level, what is the best way to choose among three different moderate-level funds? Compare their performance, using previous total returns. For example, given the three funds in Table 5-1, Fund B has the superior performance.

3) *When you want to see how well a fund has performed in comparison to market averages and other similar funds.*

Table 5-1   Choosing Relative Performance

Fund	1-Year Total Return	3-Year Annualized Total Return	5-Year Annualized Total Return
A	22.6%	10.1%	8.3%
B	13.9	15.8	14.2
C	10.7	12.9	14.1

401(k) Dilemma: Brigid's 401(k) plan offers one fund choice in each level of the pyramid. She has completed her personal pyramid and knows that she should add to either the moderate or aggressive level. She wants to know how to decide between the small-company growth fund (aggressive) and the growth and income fund (moderate).

401(k) Solution: Because these funds are in different risk levels of the pyramid, Brigid shouldn't compare them to each other, but to a group of their peers, to see how successful each is given the risk that it takes. She can choose to contribute to the best of the two, investing money outside her 401(k) plan in the level not chosen.

Two common comparison benchmarks used are the Standard & Poor's 500 Average and a peer group of funds with the same investment objective. The S&P 500 is a group of 500 U.S. stocks, tracked by the Standard & Poor Company, that represents nearly 70 percent of the total market value of U.S. stocks. The average tells you how the market performed in any given year or time period, and the information can be found in most libraries or financial newspapers. Here are some results you might expect from comparing a fund to this average:

Aggressive growth funds—Aggressive growth funds will tend to be more volatile on a year-to-year basis than the S&P 500. In a year when the S&P 500 has good performance, an aggressive fund should have better. In a year in which the S&P 500 does poorly (even negative returns for the year), an aggressive fund may be expected to do even worse. In other words, total returns tend to be more

Figure 5-1

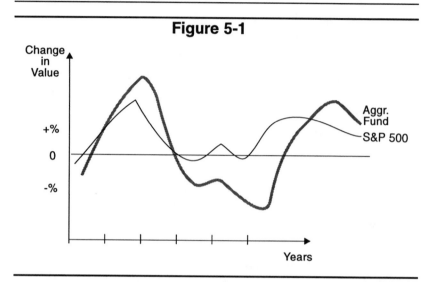

extreme than the average. (See Figure 5-1 for an example.) This short-term volatility is part of what makes them risky. A *good* aggressive growth fund will outperform the S&P 500 over the long term.

Growth funds—Growth funds strive to outperform the S&P 500 on both an annual and long-term basis. The good ones do. Their returns tend to follow the direction and volatility of the average.

Growth and income funds or balanced funds—The total returns of these funds should be less volatile than growth or aggressive growth funds. Due to the income portion of their holdings (bonds or high-yield stocks), they are cushioned in down-market years and don't take full advantage of a raging stock market in up years. A performance graph might be just the opposite of that of an aggressive fund, showing underperformance of the S&P 500 in good years and outperformance in bad. (See Figure 5-2.) Due to their ability to control risk and volatility, many balanced or

Figure 5-2

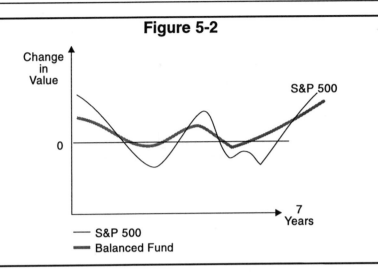

growth and income funds outperform the average over time.

Income funds—Income funds generally have no correlation to stock market averages such as the S&P 500. A better benchmark of performance for these funds is the Shearson/Lehman Bond Aggregate. Total return comparisons with either benchmark can be found in *Morningstar Mutual Funds*. (A periodical which evaluates individual mutual funds. It can be found in your local library, and is updated every two weeks.)

401(k) Tip: When checking long-term results, keep an eye out for changes in the fund manager. Don't give a new manager credit (or blame) for the previous manager's performance.

Comparing mutual funds to a group of their peers works for any investment objective and is probably one of the best ways to determine the relative success of a fund manager.

There are two sources of objective information that offer peer-group comparisons. *Morningstar Mutual Funds* ranks funds within their investment objective on a scale of 1 to 100. A score of "23" means the fund's total return ranked in the top 23 percent of all funds with the same investment objective for the time period in question. See the user's guide in the front of the publication for more in-depth information. *Value Line Mutual Funds* (A publication found in your local library, which evaluates 2,000 different mutual funds. It is updated every two weeks.) shows a +/- peer (%) figure for each period of total return given. This number shows how much better or worse the fund performed than others with a similar investment objective. For example, 2.3 means the fund's total return exceeded the peer group average by 2.3 percent. A figure of –3.8 means the fund's total return was lower than the peer group average by 3.8 percent.

***401(k)* Tip:** If your plan's funds are not publicly offered, and thus not included in one of these publications, find a fund in the publication that has the same investment objective and a similar total return number. Use that fund to see where yours *would have ranked*, had it been included in the survey.

---

3) What expenses and commissions must be paid?

In many cases, funds offered within a 401(k) plan are *no-load*, meaning there are no commissions to purchase or to sell shares. If your plan offers several public families of mutual funds, it is possible that there will be commissions involved and also possible that they will differ from family to family. (A family of funds is similar to a brand of cereal or salad dressing, with many different flavors produced by the same company.) There are even differences within a single family of funds. Fidelity Investments, for example, offers both load and no-load mutual funds.

Whether you pay a commission or load, each fund will have an expense ratio, which simply tells you how much of your total return goes to pay fund expenses. For a stock fund, a ratio of .75 percent or below is good; anything higher than 1 percent is a little excessive. For a bond or fixed-income fund, expense ratios should be well under .75 percent, with a target of .50 percent. International funds, due to the high cost of trading on foreign exchanges, may have expense ratios of 1.5 percent, which are considered acceptable.

Table 5-2 is a short mutual fund worksheet you can use to analyze and compare different funds. *Morningstar Mutual Funds* or *Value Line Mutual Funds* will have all the information needed to complete the worksheet.

Your Company's Stock

As an employee, you may be the best person *or* the worst person to analyze the prospects of your company. Ideally, you are in the best position to know how well your products are selling, whether you are reaching performance goals in terms of revenues and profits, and whether top management has a vision for the future. If you can use this knowledge when evaluating your company stock, you will probably make good, fundamentally sound decisions. On the other hand, it isn't unusual for employees, especially management, to lose their objectivity about their company. Years of indoctrination about the quality of your com-

Table 5-2 Fund Worksheet

	Fund:	Comparison to S&P 500 Index	Rank within Investment Objective
Fund			
Investment Objective			
Pyramid Level			
Morningstar Rating			
Annualized Total Returns			
1-Year			
3-Year			
5-Year			
10-Year			
Expense Ratio	12b-1 fee		
Front-End Load	Back-End Load		

pany's products or the level of its service versus the competition can diminish your ability to make impartial judgments. Selling, or even just deciding not to buy your company stock, can seem like a betrayal rather than a financial decision.

401(k) Tip: Invest in the stock of your employer due to sound fundamental reasons rather than emotional ones.

In addition to your *feel* for the direction of your company's fortunes, analyze the facts and numbers, which are available to all investors. Remember, perceptions of the investing public are a major force in determining stock prices. Ask yourself (or a trusted financial adviser) the following questions:

1) What are the prospects for the industry?

◆ Are you in the defense industry in a period of post-cold war cuts? (Not a good environment for your stock.)

◆ Are you in the auto industry, just as the economy is growing stronger? (Expect increasing revenues.)

◆ Do you expect smaller companies to have a tough time or could larger, less agile companies find it difficult to react quickly to new trends?

◆ How will the economy as a whole affect your industry? In times of economic expansion, cyclical industries such as automobile manufacturers, home and commercial builders, steel companies, and manufacturers of luxury items are expected to profit. In economic downturns, defensive industries, those whose products are consumed regardless of wealth, still pull in their revenues. Examples of such industries are beverage and food manufacturers and distributors, discount stores, and producers of home products such as detergents and toiletries.

2) What is the trend in revenues at your company?

Check your annual report, *Value Line Investment Survey*, or *Standard & Poor's Corporate Records* for last year's revenues. By looking at the quarterly numbers and computing percentage changes from year to year, you can get a good understanding of the direction of revenue growth. (Divide the difference in the two years' revenues by the earlier year's revenue to reach the percentage change.) Compare the latest year's change with three- and five-year growth rates.

◆ Is the rate of growth increasing or decreasing?

◆ How does it compare with other companies in the industry? You can find industry comparison figures in *Value Line Investment Survey*.

3) What is the trend in profits at your company?

Profits are what it's all about. How much is your company making and is it making more each year? It is important to look at profits on a per-share basis, which is called *earnings per share*, or EPS. EPS is simply the total net profit of the company divided by the number of common stock shares outstanding. Because each share of stock represents ownership of the company, the EPS figure designates the earning power of each portion of ownership. For stockholders, EPS is the most important profit figure because it tells them how much their share of the company generated in profits.

Check the growth in EPS just as you did the growth in revenues, looking at year-to-year trends and comparing the current year's growth with long-term growth.

4) What is the price/earnings ratio?

The first three questions can help you decide how well your company is performing. What they can't tell you is whether it's a good buy at the current price. The price/earnings (P/E) ratio can help you with this.

401(k) Tip: The price/earnings (P/E) ratio of a stock is its price per share divided by its earnings per share (EPS).
PRICE ÷ EPS = P/E

The ratio computes how many dollars per share you must pay for each dollar of earnings per share. If all things are equal, a lower P/E is better because you are paying less for each dollar of earnings. An analogy to comparing two stocks with the same earnings per share, but different prices, is that of shopping for two air conditioners that have the same cooling power. If one is on sale, you get more cooling power for your purchase dollar. You might consider the stock with a lower P/E ratio to be "on sale." If you hear that a stock is selling "at a discount to the market," it has a lower P/E than the average stock.

Why would anyone be willing to buy stocks with high P/E ratios? Because they expect earnings growth, as shown in the following 401(k) Dilemma.

401(k) Dilemma: The Cushing Couch Company stock has a price of $40 per share and EPS of $2 per share. Its P/E ratio is $40 ÷ $2 = **20**. A competitor, the Capshaw Couch Company, also has EPS of $2 per share, but its stock price is $60. Its P/E ratio is $60 ÷ $2 = **30**.

Why would anyone be willing to buy the Capshaw Couch Company stock at $60 when they could get the same $2 in earnings per share with the Cushing Couch Company for just $40?

Probably because they believe that the EPS at Capshaw will soon grow. If the EPS grows to $3 per share, its P/E ratio will be 20 ($60 ÷ $3 = 20), the same as the P/E ratio for Cushing.

What is the danger? That those $3 earnings don't materialize as expected. Then, to bring its P/E into line with Cushing's and other companies in their industry, Capshaw's stock price would have to drop from $60 to $40.

To find out whether your company's P/E ratio is high, average, or low when compared to other stocks, check its relative P/E ratio in *Value Line Investment Survey*, which compares a stock's P/E to all others in the survey. A ratio of one is average; more than one shows a relatively high ratio; and less than one, a low ratio. If your company stock isn't in their universe, check *Investors' Business Daily*, which publishes the average P/E ratio of the Dow Jones Industrial Average for a comparison figure.

Another rule of thumb compares the P/E ratio with the rate of growth in earnings per share. Following the concept that high P/Es are a result of expected growth in EPS, it contends that a company's P/E ratio should not be higher than its rate of growth in EPS. For example, a P/E ratio of 35 might not be considered too high for a company whose EPS is growing at the rate of 50 percent per year, but the same 35 P/E is considered high for a company whose annual EPS growth is 15 percent.

5) What are the ROE and ROA?

Return on equity (ROE) and *Return on assets* (ROA) are measures of total return for the company, very similar to the measures of total return you use to gauge the performance of your investments. Both of these ratios calculate the money returned (profits) on the money invested (equity or assets). Your annual report or any independent information source should have both of these ratios calculated for you. Analyze the numbers in two ways:

◆ Compare to other companies in the same industry

◆ Compare year-to-year figures and trends

Higher is better, and an increasing trend is a positive sign.

Use the worksheet in Table 5-3 to analyze your company stock.

Annuities

An annuity is a contract with an insurance company that offers deferral of taxes on capital gains and income until you withdraw the funds. If your plan's investment options are annuities, your research and analysis task is very similar to that of a plan offering mutual funds. There is one striking difference, however, and that is the safety of the insurance company providing the annuities. Because insurance companies are not just in the investment business but also in the property and casualty and life insurance business, they have many unknown risks and claims against their assets. This adds a different dimension to analyzing the risk of an annuity. Before investigating the particular annuity fund, its past performance, and fees,

Table 5-3   Stock Worksheet

Company _____
Stock Exchange _____
Current Price _____
Dividend per Share $ _____
P/E Ratio _____

Symbol _____
52 Week High and Low _____
Dividend Yield _____
Relative P/E Ratio _____

Value Line Rankings (if available)

Timeliness 1 2 3 4 5
Safety   1 2 3 4 5

Annual Rates of Change			
	One Year	Three Years	Five Years	+/- Industry Average
Revenues				
Earnings per Share				
Dividends				

Return on Equity _____ Trend _____ Industry _____
Return on Assets _____ Trend _____ Industry _____

you must check out the strength and stability of the insurance company that issues it.

Three companies—A.M. Best, Moody's Investor Services, and Standard & Poor's—all rate insurance companies. Call the reference room of your local library or Standard & Poor's (212-553-0377) for the rating of any insurance company. A rating less than an "A" means that there are additional risks to investing your money with this company.

401(k) Tip: You should check this rating annually, because circumstances and financial stability can change. Don't be the last to know that your insurance company is having difficulties.

Once you are comfortable with the insurance company, begin to look at the different annuities offered within your plan. There are two basic types: fixed and variable.

Fixed annuities are similar in *structure* (not risk—CDs are FDIC-insured while annuities are not) to a certificate of deposit. You are guaranteed a particular rate of return for a certain time period. At the end of that time period, you can renew at the current rate available.

Advantages: You will always know the rate of return. Unless the insurance company becomes insolvent, your account will not lose money.

Disadvantages: As with any fixed-rate investment, you are not protected against inflation. For this reason, fixed annuities are not recommended for long-term retirement accounts. If you do invest in fixed annuities, beware of initial "teaser" rates, which entice new investors but are not available to existing annuity-holders. Upon renewal, you may find that your interest rate is much less attractive.

$$ Money Mistake: Genny had the option of choosing from two different annuity companies in her plan. Because she was nearing retirement, she decided on a fixed annuity. She chose Company A because its one-year fixed rate was 7 percent, while Company B's rate was only 6.5 percent.

When it came time to renew at the end of one year, her renewal rate had dropped to only 6 percent, while the renewal rates at Company B were still 6.5 percent. What was her mistake?

Choosing a company with high "teaser" rates can seem smart at the time, but doing so can set you up for disappointment later. Existing policyholders can expect lower rates of return, which pay for the high returns being given to new customers. Always ask about rates given to current customers.

Variable annuities are very much like mutual funds in their design. They include a pooled set of investments, which are grouped according to investment objective and whose value is subject to the market value of the underlying securities. Unlike a fixed annuity, there is no guarantee of investment returns.

Just as with a mutual fund, begin your analysis with investment objectives. Complete your personal pyramid, compare it to the recommendations for your financial stage of life, and decide where (which level of the pyramid) you need to add. If you have to, shift your non-retirement investments around so that you can invest 401(k) or

403(b) funds in the growth levels (moderate and aggressive) of the pyramid.

After you have chosen your pyramid level and narrowed your choices to a few investment objectives, begin analyzing past performance. Do this in the same way we studied performance for mutual funds, with one difference. Your independent source of information will be *Morningstar Variable Annuity/and Life*, a publication that should be available in your library and is updated every two weeks.

Advantages: Variable annuities offer growth potential and many different investment choices.

Disadvantages: Rates of return are not guaranteed and values may fluctuate with market conditions.

See Table 5-4 for an annuity worksheet.

Summary

As you analyze your investment options, remember the following rules:

- ◆ Stay on track. A retirement plan is a long-term venture and you won't get where you want to go using short-term vehicles. As the popular investment company advertisement says, "No one plans to fail, they just fail to plan." Make your money work as hard as you do, and take advantage of the power of time.

- ◆ Keep some growth investments in your portfolio. Over the past 60 years, stocks have averaged around 10 percent annualized return, while long-term bonds have lagged behind at 5 percent, and Treasury bills

Table 5-4 Annuity Worksheet

Annuity	
Issuing Insurance Co.	
Company Rating	
Investment Objective	
Pyramid Level	
Morningstar Rating	

Annuity:	Comparison to S&P 500 Index or LB Gov't/Corp	Rank within Investment Objective
Annualized Total Returns		
1-Year		
3-Year		
5-Year		
10-Year		

Surrender Charges	Front-End Load	
Contract Charge	M&E Risk Charge	
Administration Fee	Management Fee	

turned in a 4 percent return. Growth protects against inflation and is critical to balancing your portfolio. The markets are certain to move up and down over the years, but over the long term, growth investments win the race.

◆ Collect all the available information about an investment *before* you spend your hard-earned money. Never invest in something you do not completely understand.

◆ Diversify among your investment options. Spreading out your retirement dollars and making periodic changes will help to secure the suitable asset mix you need.

Chapter Six

How Much Money Will You Need?

"Retirement is coming! Retirement is coming!" You read about it in the newspaper, see it on television, and hear it on the radio. Does this cry echo the crazy panic of Chicken Little, or the valuable warning of Paul Revere? The answer depends on how much you will need in retirement. If you are saving enough now, those chants may seem to say, "The sky is falling," when it isn't. But, if like many, your retirement needs outweigh your current planning and saving, you had better listen to Paul.

One difficulty of retirement planning is its parameters—an undetermined amount of money, to last an undetermined length of time, in a highly volatile financial environment including changes in costs of living, medical costs, taxes, and Social Security laws.

Is it possible to know just how much you will need in retirement? Unfortunately, it isn't. There are many variables, just some of which we list below:

◆ Your lifestyle and its costs

◆ The age at which you retire

◆ When you begin retirement investing

◆ How long you will live

◆ The state of Social Security

◆ Taxation of Social Security

◆ Your company pension benefits

◆ The total return on your retirement savings

◆ The rate of inflation

◆ Marginal income tax rates

◆ Changes in 401(k), 403(b), and IRA laws

Understanding these variables, especially those that you can control, is the first step in realizing a sensible savings plan for retirement. Let's start with the first variable: your lifestyle.

Your Lifestyle and Its Costs

Michelle and Steve have four children, all of whom live within 20 miles of their home. They are devoted grandparents and prefer entertaining in their home to vacationing in exotic locales. Meg and Kurt have three children, two of whom are in graduate school on opposite coasts. Having worked, saved, and sacrificed during their children's growing years, they look forward to a retirement that includes travel and a winter home in a warmer climate. Will these two couples need the same amount of money to support their chosen lifestyle in retirement? Probably not.

Decide now what your retirement lifestyle will be, so that your financial situation doesn't decide for you during retirement. Don't let a lack of planning dictate how you spend a much-deserved rest.

There are two ways to compute how much annual income you may need, one of which takes into account your current lifestyle, then estimates the future, and another attempts to calculate future expenses. They may or may not arrive at similar numbers. We recommend you try both, beginning with the arbitrary percentage measure, which is certainly easier.

401(k) Tip: A general rule-of-thumb calculates retirement income needs at 75 percent of current income.

The reasoning behind lower cash requirements in retirement comes from reduced costs in some or all of the following current expense categories:

◆ Commuting

◆ Business wardrobe

◆ Business meals

◆ Taxes

◆ Retirement saving

◆ Mortgage or auto, when payments are completed

If you expect your life to include extensive travel plans, a wish to help your children or grandchildren financially, a retirement home in a more desirable climate, or other expensive hobbies or activities, a figure nearer to 100 percent of pre-retirement income may be more accurate.

To create a more exact figure, compute each of your current expenses as a percentage of your income, just as you would when determining a budget. Deduct the costs that you will no longer incur, make reductions in those that will exist to a lesser extent, add expenses that you expect but do not incur now, and estimate your necessary income from there. If you are undecided, it is best to err on the conservative side, choosing a higher expected income requirement.

The Age at Which You Retire

You may be 50 or you may be 70. You may wish you could retire tomorrow or you may not want to retire at all. Whatever your plans, the age at which you and/or your spouse leave your full-time job(s) has a significant impact on your retirement planning. There are three things that happen if you choose to retire earlier rather than later.

1) The sooner you begin drawing Social Security benefits, the smaller the amount you will receive annually.

Under current law, the normal retirement age (the age at which you can receive full benefits) is 65. In the future, the age will increase until it reaches age 67 for individuals born in 1960 or later. See Table 6-1 to see if you will be affected. Under current law, you can receive benefits as early as 62, but the benefits will not equal your full retirement benefit. See Table 6-2 to see how the percentages change.

2) For each year in which you do not earn an income, you cannot add to your retirement savings.

3) For each year in which you do not earn an income, you reduce your retirement savings by your living expenses for that year.

The second two items combined can really make a difference over just a few years.

Table 6-1

Year of Birth	Normal Retirement Age (Full Benefits)	
	Years	Months*
1937 or before	65	
1938	65	2
1939	65	4
1940	65	6
1941	65	8
1942	65	10
1943-1954	66	
1955	66	2
1956	66	4
1957	66	6
1958	66	8
1959	66	10
1960 or later	67	

65 years and 8 months is normal retirement age.

Table 6-2   Changes in Social Security Benefits Based on Retirement Age

Retirement Age	Percentage of Full Benefit*
62	80
63	86.7
64	93.3
65	100
66	104.5
67	109
68	113.5

*For people who turn 65 in 1994, add 4.5 percent per year for every year you delay retirement. The rate gradually increases in future years, until it reaches 8 percent per year for those who turn 65 in 2008 or later.

401(k) Dilemma: Greg is 60, earns $50,000 per year, and saves $4,500 each year for retirement. He is trying to decide whether to retire this year or next. He estimates that his annual retirement expenses will be approximately $40,000. What will be the difference in his financial situation if he retires now?

Annual living expenses withdrawn from savings $40,000
Savings not deposited to his retirement fund ___4,500
Cost of retiring this year rather than next year $44,500

Now consider what that $44,500 could earn in his retirement account in the future. After 10 years at 8 percent total return, that $44,500 would be worth $96,072. That makes an expensive year of retirement.

When You Begin Retirement Investing

It is never too early or too late to start building a retirement nest egg. Obviously, the earlier you can start saving, the better; the more you will have later. Just looking at the numbers should convince you to get on the road to saving as soon as possible.

401(k) Dilemma: Megan and Brian work for the same company and are 25 years old. They are both eligible for their 401(k) plan, but disagree about when they should start investing. Brian doesn't think he can afford 401(k) contributions right now and has decided to wait 10 years, until age 35, and then begin investing the same as Megan. Megan wants to begin right away investing

$2,000 annually, but stop contributing in 10 years. Considering the two scenarios, who will have accumulated the most money at age 65 assuming an 8 percent average total return and identical tax situations?

If you said Megan, you were right. Due to the power of compounding, she would collect $291,547 on contributions of just $20,000. Starting later, Brian would only have $226,566 after contributing $60,000. You can see that your money works much harder when you give it more time to grow.

How Long You Will Live

This may seem morbid, but it isn't designed so much to elicit anxiety as to make you realize that people are living longer these days, and it isn't unlikely that you and/or your spouse will live past the age of 80. Realizing that, consider how much money it will take to support you, post-retirement, for 20 or 30 years.

The State of Social Security

You don't have to look far for reports that our Social Security system exists on borrowed time. As the Baby Boomer population ages, experts predict that there will be only two tax-paying workers for every one benefit-collecting retiree. Right now, that number is over three. Expectations are that many in this generation will pay much more into the system in the form of Social Security taxes than they will ever collect in benefits.

To find out how much you can expect to receive under our current system, contact your local Social Security Administration office, or call (800) 772-1213 for a copy of form SSA-7004-PC-OPC, *Request for Earnings and Benefit Estimate Statement*. You should complete this form every three years to check for any errors that have been made in reporting your income. You only have three years to correct an error, after which time all reported information becomes a permanent part of your record. If your income was under-reported by mistake, your future benefits will be based on an amount of income (and Social Security taxes paid) which is lower than it should be.

Table 6-3 shows estimates of average Social Security benefits.

Table 6-3   Approximate Monthly Benefits at Full Retirement Age

Your Age in 1994	Your Family	Your Earnings in 1993				
		$20,000	**$30,000**	**$40,000**	**$50,000**	**$57,600+**
45	You	$ 777	$1,044	$1,177	$1,301	$1,400
	You & Spouse	1,165	1,566	1,765	1,953	2,100
55	You	777	1,043	1,157	1,244	1,302
	You & Spouse	1,165	1,564	1,753	1,866	1,953
65	You	752	998	1,076	1,127	1,147
	You & Spouse	1,128	1,497	1,616	1,690	1,720

Your actual benefits will be based on your past earnings, but this chart can give you an estimate, assuming that you had a steady lifetime of earnings.

Your spouse is assumed to be the same age. He or she may qualify for a higher retirement benefit based on his or her own work record.

Taxation of Social Security

According to the Social Security Administration, about 20 percent of people who receive Social Security benefits pay taxes on their benefits now. In addition to possible taxes on your benefits, you can be penalized for earning an income while receiving Social Security payments. Table 6-4 shows loss of benefit for each dollar of earnings in retirement. To learn more, call your local IRS office or the national toll-free number, 1-800-829-3676, for Publication 554, *Tax Information for Older Americans.*

While it would be political suicide for Congress to abolish Social Security, upper-income recipients are under fire. Those arguing against benefits for the wealthy (or even the relatively comfortable) disregard the thousands of dollars in taxes they have paid, stating simply that they have less need for the income due to other savings and investments. Given the state of the deficit and political sentiment toward raising taxes, be prepared to pay more in taxes on your Social Security income than current recipients, especially if you are in an upper-income bracket; expect to see benefits reduced at lower thresholds of earned income.

Table 6-4

Ages*	Annual Exempt Amount	Benefit Withheld for Each Dollar Earned over Exempt Amount
Under 65	$7,680	$.50
65 to 69	$10,560	$.33
70 or older	none	none

*1994 limits.

Your Company Pension Benefits

As defined-benefit pension plans have been replaced by employee contribution plans such as 401(k)s, it is less common to receive a certain percentage of your salary as a pension for your retirement. If you are lucky enough to have a pension plan, ask your employer about the level of benefits you can expect. Check vesting periods if you are considering a new job. You may find that remaining with your current employer is in your best interest, financially. If you are married and either you or your spouse has a pension plan, check into spousal benefits, should the primary beneficiary die.

The Total Return on Your Retirement Savings

The average total return on your investments can make a big difference in how much money you will have available at retirement. While investments with higher total returns generally have more risk and more volatility (see the discussion of the investment pyramid in Chapter 3), the long-term nature of retirement planning allows you to weather any storm. To see how just a few percentage points difference in total return can make a big difference in dollars earned, see Table 6-5.

The Rate of Inflation

Your biggest enemy in long-range investment planning is inflation. What you are really striving for is not a certain sum of money, but a level of consumption, the ability to maintain a particular lifestyle. This is best described as

Table 6-5   Total Return and Your Retirement Fund— How Much Will You Have at Age 65?

Average Annual Total Return	Beginning Age / Investing $200 Each Month*			
	25	35	45	55
3 percent	$ 185,675	$116,839	$65,825	$28,018
5 percent	306,476	167,145	82,549	31,186
8 percent	702,856	300,059	118,589	36,833
10 percent	1,275,356	455,865	153,139	41,310
15 percent	6,280,751	1,401,964	303,191	55,731

*Investments made at the beginning of the month.

purchasing power rather than dollars. The fact that purchasing power and fixed dollars are not the same can be attributed to inflation (or, in rare instances, deflation). In a world where the annual inflation rate is 5 percent, it will take $1.05 next year to buy what $1.00 will buy today. A nickel may not seem like much, but check Table 6-6 to see that, over 20 years, 5 percent inflation can reduce the purchasing power of $1.00 to just $.38.

The argument for investing your long-term retirement funds in growth investments has much to do with inflation and the concept of *real returns*. The real return on an investment is its total return less the rate of inflation.

401(k) Tip: Total Return – Inflation Rate = Real Return

For example, if you have an investment such as a growth or balanced mutual fund whose total return (dividends or interest + price change) is 10 percent, while the rate of inflation is 5 percent, its real return is 5 percent (10% – 5% = 5%). If you have another investment, such as a money market account whose total return is 3 percent,

Table 6-6   What Will $1.00 Be Worth?

Years from Today	Rate of Inflation					
	3 %	5 %	6 %	8 %	10 %	15 %
5	$0.86	$0.78	$0.75	$0.68	$0.62	$0.50
6	0.84	0.75	0.70	0.63	0.56	0.43
7	0.81	0.71	0.65	0.58	0.51	0.38
8	0.79	0.68	0.63	0.54	0.47	0.33
9	0.77	0.64	0.59	0.50	0.42	0.28
10	0.74	0.61	0.56	0.46	0.39	0.25
15	0.64	0.48	0.42	0.32	0.24	0.12
20	0.55	0.38	0.31	0.21	0.15	0.06
25	0.48	0.30	0.23	0.15	0.09	0.03
30	0.41	0.23	0.17	0.10	0.06	0.02
35	0.36	0.18	0.13	0.07	0.04	0.01
40	0.31	0.14	0.10	0.05	0.02	<0.01
45	0.26	0.11	0.07	0.03	0.01	<0.01
50	0.23	0.09	0.05	0.02	0.01	<0.01

its real return is –2 percent (3% – 5% = –2%). The argument for growth investments follows the concept that many low-return, fixed-income investments, while considered *safe*, can have negative real returns. After inflation, you can lose purchasing power.

Marginal Income Tax Rates

Changes in marginal tax rates could have a significant effect on your retirement if you are currently investing in a 401(k) or 403(b) plan and/or IRAs. Because you do not pay current income taxes on the funds invested in a 401(k) or 403(b) plan (and in some instances, IRAs), and you also do not pay current income taxes on capital gains and income earned by those funds, you must pay taxes during retirement, when you withdraw. If you are 20 years from retirement, there isn't much you can do, so don't worry about it. However, if you are just a few years from retirement and are older than 59½, you can make adjustments. Tax hikes generally are not sprung upon us, but are accompanied by much political posturing, which allows plenty of time to make changes in your strategy (watch out for retroactive increases). It may be worthwhile to withdraw funds from IRAs and 401(k) or 403(b) plans ahead of an increase in marginal income tax rates to avoid paying additional income taxes.

401(k) Tip: Make sure that your withdrawal doesn't bump you into a higher tax bracket, thereby eliminating the advantage.

Changes in 401(k), 403(b), and IRA Laws

As we have moved from a time in which all IRAs were tax-deductible to a time in which, based on income and employer-provided savings plans, only some are, future changes are certainly possible. Why? The tax break you receive takes spending money out of Congress' pockets. Don't lose sleep over the possibility, but prepare to write your congressional representative if you hear talk of eliminating tax-deferred plans.

Don't let all these variables discourage you. They don't mean that you can't devise a reasonable plan to save for a comfortable retirement. What they do mean is that you can't figure it out once and then stay on auto-pilot.

Each year, you should recalculate your retirement situation to make sure you are on track.

Using worksheets to calculate what you will need

Tables 6-7, 6-8, and 6-9 can help you to calculate how much you will need and how much to save until then, using 20-, 25-, and 30-year retirement periods. The assumptions are:

◆ Inflation averages 5 percent

◆ Savings and investments grow at 10 percent (you'll need growth investments)

◆ Principal will be depleted after retirement

For example, if you have 10 years until retirement, use the Factors Chart to obtain an Inflation Factor of 1.63, a Growth Factor of 2.59, and a Savings Factor of 15.94.

Summary

There is no foolproof method of calculating exactly how much retirement saving is enough. However, by understanding the variables and making changes accordingly, you can make educated plans for a comfortable retirement.

Because the assumptions we use may differ from real life, use the retirement worksheets as a starting point, not as the final word on how much you should save. They may be most helpful in making decisions about early retirement; use the three different worksheets to estimate a different starting point and length of retirement.

Table 6-7 20-Year 401(k) Retirement Worksheet

1. Current Gross Salary		
(75 percent needed to maintain lifestyle in retirement)	x	.75
2. Retirement Income Needed to Maintain Lifestyle	=	
3. Inflation Adjustment Factor (from table below)	x	
4. Inflation Adjusted Retirement Income Needed	=	
5. Estimated Pension Plan Income		
6. Estimated Social Security Income	+	
7. Total Retirement Benefit Income (#5 plus #6)	=	
8. Additional Income Needed (#4 minus #7)		
9. Capital Required to Generate Additional Income	x	13.99 *
Needed	=	
10. Total Current Retirement Savings		
11. Growth Factor (from table below)	x	
12. Value of Current Savings at Retirement	=	
13. Additional Capital Needed at Retirement (#9 minus #12)		
14. Divided by Savings Factor (from table below)		
15. Annual Savings Needed to Accumulate Additional Capital	=	

GROWTH AND SAVINGS FACTORS

Factor	Years to Retirement			
	5	10	15	20
Inflation	1.28	1.63	2.08	2.65
Growth	1.61	2.59	4.18	6.73
Savings	6.11	15.94	31.77	57.28

Assumptions: Inflation averages 5 percent; savings and investments grow at 10 percent; annual income required during retirement grows by 5 percent annually to allow for inflation; retirement lasts 20 years; and principal will be depleted after 20 years.

*The 13.99 factor used to generate capital required for 20 years of retirement includes the assumption that investments will continue to grow at 10 perent and that annual income required grows by 5 percent annually to allow for inflation.

Table 6-8   25-Year 401(k) Retirement Worksheet

1. Current Gross Salary		
(75 percent needed to maintain lifestyle in retirement)	x	.75
2. Retirement Income Needed to Maintain Lifestyle	=	
3. Inflation Adjustment Factor (from table below)	x	
4. Inflation Adjusted Retirement Income Needed	=	
5. Estimated Pension Plan Income		
6. Estimated Social Security Income	+	
7. Total Retirement Benefit Income (#5 plus #6)	=	
8. Additional Income Needed (#4 minus #7)		
9. Capital Required to Generate Additional Income	x	15.88 *
Needed	=	
10. Total Current Retirement Savings		
11. Growth Factor (from table below)	x	
12. Value of Current Savings at Retirement	=	
13. Additional Capital Needed at Retirement (#9 minus #12)		
14. Divided by Savings Factor (from table below)		
15. Annual Savings Needed to Accumulate Additional Capital	=	

GROWTH AND SAVINGS FACTORS

Factor	Years to Retirement			
	5	10	15	20
Inflation	1.28	1.63	2.08	2.65
Growth	1.61	2.59	4.18	6.73
Savings	6.11	15.94	31.77	57.28

Assumptions: Inflation averages 5 percent; savings and investments grow at 10 percent; annual income required during retirement grows by 5 percent annually to allow for inflation, retirement lasts 25 years; and principal will be depleted after 25 years.

*The 15.88 factor used to generate capital required for 20 years of retirement includes the assumption that investments will continue to grow at 10 perent and that annual income required grows by 5 percent annually to allow for inflation.

Table 6-9   30-Year 401(k) Retirement Worksheet

1. Current Gross Salary		
(75 percent needed to maintain lifestyle in retirement)	x	.75
2. Retirement Income Needed to Maintain Lifestyle	=	
3. Inflation Adjustment Factor (from table below)	x	
4. Inflation Adjusted Retirement Income Needed	=	
5. Estimated Pension Plan Income		
6. Estimated Social Security Income	+	
7. Total Retirement Benefit Income (#5 plus #6)	=	
8. Additional Income Needed (#4 minus #7)		
9. Capital Required to Generate Additional Income	x	17.38*
Needed	=	
10. Total Current Retirement Savings		
11. Growth Factor (from table below)	x	
12. Value of Current Savings at Retirement	=	
13. Additional Capital Needed at Retirement (#9 minus #12)		
14. Divided by Savings Factor (from table below)		
15. Annual Savings Needed to Accumulate Additional Capital	=	

GROWTH AND SAVINGS FACTORS

	Years to Retirement			
Factor	5	10	15	20
Inflation	1.28	1.63	2.08	2.65
Growth	1.61	2.59	4.18	6.73
Savings	6.11	15.94	31.77	57.28

Assumptions: Inflation averages 5 percent; savings and investments grow at 10 percent; annual income required during retirement grows by 5 percent annually to allow for inflation, retirement lasts 30 years; and principal will be depleted after 30 years.

*The 17.38 factor used to generate capital required for 20 years of retirement includes the assumption that investments will continue to grow at 10 perent and that annual income required grows by 5 percent annually to allow for inflation.

Chapter Seven
401(k)/403(b), IRA, or Both?

Nancy and Jeff are in their mid-thirties, have just purchased a home, and are beginning to think seriously about
putting some money away for retirement. They have been
approached by several financial planners and are some-
what confused by the differing advice. Their employers
encourage them to invest in company-sponsored 401(k)
plans and investment salespeople are pushing IRAs, annuities, and insurance products. Their question to us was,
"Should we start our retirement savings with an IRA or
our 401(k) plans, or should we invest in mutual funds,
insurance, or annuities?" We told them that their retirement savings should be accumulated in this order:

401(k)/403(b) plan

↓

IRA, deductible or not

↓

Tax-deferred investments, such as annuities (maybe)

↓

Ordinary growth investments, such as mutual funds

You should move down a level (i.e., from 401(k)/403(b)
to IRA or IRA to annuities) only when you have invested

the maximum annual amount allowed by law in the previous level. Some people may choose to skip the annuities level altogether.

$$ Note: The discussion of annuities in this chapter pertains to their purchase outside a 401(k) or 403(b) plan.

Maximum 401(k) Contributions

By law, you can save up to a maximum, pre-tax contribution of $9,240 (1994 rules) in your 401(k) plan. The maximum combined employee and employer contribution is the lesser of $30,000 or 25 percent of your annual compensation. You may reach your maximum well before the IRS limit, due to your plan limits. For example, if your plan allows you to contribute a maximum of 10 percent of your $30,000 salary, the most you can contribute to your 401(k) account each year is $3,000, not $9,240. If your employer matches 50 percent ($1,500) of your contributions, the upper limit to your combined deposits is $4,500, not $30,000. 403(b) plan limits are essentially the same, subject to a few exceptions that allow higher contributions. (Read more in Chapter 1 or in IRS Publication 571.)

Because your 401(k) plan allows the maximum tax advantage for retirement saving (IRA contributions may or may not be tax-deductible, and annuity and insurance contracts only offer tax-deferral on growth), be sure to exhaust your opportunity for investing in the 401(k) plan before looking at other retirement options. Once you have reached the limit to your 401(k) contribution, it is time to take a look at the next level, IRAs.

401(k) Dilemma: Amy is divorced, in her mid-forties, her children have left the nest, and she has no retirement savings. She has just joined her 401(k) plan and is contributing the 10 percent maximum that her plan allows. Her salary is $25,000 and she contributes $2,500 each year. Her biggest concern right now is saving enough to be able to retire comfortably.

What should she do? She should plan to open an IRA. The IRS can tell her whether her contribution will be tax-deductible. Under 1993 rules, as a single person with a salary of $25,000, she is eligible for a deduction (see Table 7-1). This would allow her to defer taxes on an additional $2,000 per year, plus the taxes on any investment growth. Even if the $2,000 is more than she is able to put away each year, any amount up to the $2,000 will move her closer to her retirement goals.

IRAs—Individual Retirement Accounts

If you have invested the maximum allowable in your 401(k) plan but know that you will need more savings for retirement, consider opening an IRA or adding to an existing account. No matter what your income, tax filing status, or other retirement plan options, each year you can contribute $2,000 or your total earned income, whichever is lower, to an IRA. If you have a non-working spouse, together you can contribute $2,250 to two IRAs, in any combination, as long as neither account receives more than $2,000 per year. For example, you may contribute $1,125 to each account or $1,000 to one and $1,250 to the other.

401(k) Tip: Robert wanted to open an IRA last year, but couldn't because he didn't have $2,000 on April 15th. He decided that this year he would contribute each month instead of trying to do it all at once. He started saving $166.00 per month and will easily reach his goal of $2,000. Take the sting out of writing big checks by saving a little at a time.

If you invest in an IRA, the rules are comparable to the rules in your 401(k) plan.

◆ If you withdraw money before the age of 59½, you must pay a 10 percent IRS penalty.

◆ At any time you withdraw money, all or some of it will be subject to current income taxes, depending on whether your contributions were deductible or non-deductible.

◆ You must begin withdrawing your money by April 1 of the year following the year in which you turn 70½.

IRAs—Deductible or not?

Check Table 7-1 to see whether, under 1993 rules, you can deduct the amount of an IRA contribution from your income when computing your income taxes. Call the IRS to find out whether the limits have changed for 1994 and beyond. If you find out that you cannot deduct an IRA, is it still worth having one? The answer depends on how you weigh the benefit of tax-deferred growth with lack of liquidity. Even without an immediate tax deduction, you can benefit from the fact that current earnings on your investments are not subject to income taxes.

Table 7-1 Can You Deduct an IRA?

If Your Adjusted Gross Income Is		If You Are Covered by a Retirement Plan at Work and Your Filing Status Is			If You Are Not Covered by a Retirement Plan at Work and Your Filing Status Is			
		Single or Head of Household	Married, filing jointly (even if your spouse is not covered by a plan at work) / Qualifying Widow(er)	Married, filing separately	Married, filing jointly (and your spouse is covered by a plan at work)	Single or Head of Household	Married, filing jointly or separately (and your spouse is not covered by a plan at work) / Qualifying Widow(er)	Married, filing separately (even if your spouse is covered by a plan at work)
At Least	But Less Than	You Can Take	You Can Take	You Can Take	You Can Take	You Can Take	You Can Take	You Can Take
$0-	$10,000	Full deduction	Full deduction	Part deduction	Full deduction			
$10,000	$25,000	Full deduction	Full deduction	No deduction	Full deduction		Full deduction	
$25,000	$35,000	Part deduction	Full deduction	No deduction	Full deduction	Full deduction		Full deduction
$35,000	$40,000	No deduction	Full deduction	No deduction	Full deduction			
$40,000	$50,000	No deduction	Part deduction	No deduction	Part deduction			
$50,000 or over		No deduction	No deduction	No deduction	No deduction			

For example, if you have $1,000 invested and it earns 8 percent ($80) in one year, you pay income taxes on the $80 if the investment is not in a tax-deferred account; if it is, you pay no taxes now. In the following year, you would have the full $1,080 invested in a tax-deferred account, but just $1,057.60 ($1,080 less 28 percent taxes on the $80 income) in a regular account. See Table 7-2 to see how the tax-deferral increases the money you keep in just three years. Table 7-3 shows how the small difference reached in Table 7-2 can grow over 20 years. Even without the benefit of tax deductibility, you keep more money when it grows tax-deferred.

Table 7-2 Tax-Deferred Investments

	Ordinary Investment	Tax-Deferred Investment
Initial investment	$1,000.00	$1,000.00
8% income, year one	80.00	80.00
Current income tax at 28%	(22.40)	0.00
Net principal result	1,057.60	1,080.00
8% income, year two	84.61	86.40
Current income tax at 28%	(23.69)	0.00
Net principal result	1,118.52	1,166.40
8% income, year three	89.48	93.31
Current income tax at 28%	(25.05)	0.00
Net principal result	1,182.95	1,259.71
Tax on withdrawal at 28%	0.00	72.72
The money you keep	**$1,182.95**	**$1,186.99**

Table 7-3 Tax-Deferred Investments

	Ordinary Investment	Tax-Deferred Investment
Initial investment	$2,000	$2,000
Value after 20 years at 8% Ordinary investment income taxed at 28% annually	6,130	9,322
Income tax on withdrawal (growth of account = $7,322) at 28%	$0	($2,050)
The money you keep	**$6,130**	**$7,272**

401(k) Tip: If you invest in a non-deductible IRA, you will only be taxed on the growth of the account at withdrawal, not the entire account value. Because the amount you initially invested has already been subject to taxes, only the amount in excess of your original investment will be taxed. To avoid any confusion upon withdrawal, do not combine deductible and non-deductible IRAs.

Investing your IRA

Deciding to save money through an IRA is easy, but if you want the most out of your money you must invest well. Begin with your personal pyramid: know exactly where you are. Keeping in mind that long-term retirement funds are best invested in the growth (moderate and aggressive) levels of the pyramid, compare your personal pyramid to your goal pyramid and decide where you need to add or subtract. If you find that you are under-weighted in either of the bottom two (conservative or most conservative) levels, consider moving some of your non-retirement funds to these levels so that retirement funds can be invested in the growth levels (moderate and aggressive). Why not take maximum advantage of the benefit of tax-deferral by investing for higher return in your retirement accounts?

$$ Money Mistake: It is a rare occasion in which we would recommend investing your retirement funds in the speculative level. Primarily because you do not want to be careless with your retirement funds—the speculative level is the place for "play money." Additionally, there is the practical thought that if you insist on investing in speculative investments, in many cases you will lose some or all of your money. And if you do lose, at least you can take a tax deduction for the loss if the investment is not in a tax-deferred account.

Investing in mutual funds

Once you are ready to proceed to the "How to Get There" stage, consider several different types of investments to fill the gaps in your personal pyramid. Because they offer professional management, diversification of risk, and can be purchased in small amounts, mutual funds are an excellent way to invest your IRA. Check them out in *Value Line Mutual Funds* or *Morningstar Mutual Funds*. Both sources offer easy-to-read, independent information and performance analyses about many different funds. Use the information you can garner from either source, read Chapter 4 for more about analyzing different investments, and complete the mutual fund worksheet (Table 5-2). The format of the worksheet will help you digest all the data, compare funds, and monitor their progress.

Most mutual fund companies can open an IRA account for you with little or no additional cost. Make sure that the form you complete states that you are opening an IRA account. Using the wrong form can keep your account from being treated as an IRA, even though *you* intended for it to be an IRA. Some errors are not reversible, so be very careful when you complete the paperwork.

Investing in stocks

If you are willing to spend a significant amount of time on your investments and you have a fairly large amount ($50,000 or more) of money in your IRA, you may want to use a *self-directed IRA*, which allows you to purchase individual stocks and bonds. Any brokerage firm and most banks can open such an account. The annual maintenance fees are relatively low—$35 to $50 per year—and many firms run specials that require no fee for establishing the account. Use *Value Line Investment Survey* to complete the stock worksheet (Table 5-3), if you are investigating different stocks. Begin by choosing an industry that you feel has strong growth potential, then research several companies within the industry to find one or two with the strongest record of revenue, earnings, dividends, and earnings-per-share growth. Keep in mind that diversifying among different companies can protect you from a disaster at any one.

40I(k) Tip: Always hold several different stocks in several different industries; never keep all your eggs in one basket. Remember *The Rule of Five:* For every five stocks you purchase, three will perform as expected, one will have stellar performance, and one will be your worst nightmare. Choose all five, and the return of the good performers will cover any losses on the "dogs." Choose only one, and which one will it be? It could be the nightmare.

Investing in bonds

A bond is simply a formal I.O.U. issued by a corporation, government agency, or municipality. In exchange for the use of your money, the institution that issues the bond will pay you interest until returning your money to you. Bonds have stated maturity dates, generally pay interest semi-annually, and usually come in denominations of $1,000 or more. For example, a $1,000, 8 percent bond due in 2010 would pay its owner $80 every year until 2010, when it would pay the face value, or $1,000. All of this would occur as planned, provided that the company or entity issuing the bonds remained financially viable. You can check the financial strength of a corporation or municipality by finding its Standard & Poor's or Moody's Investors Service rating in your local library or from your investment broker. Any rating at or above BBB (S&P) or Baa (Moody's) is considered investment grade.

If you are interested in bonds, consider *convertible bonds* for your IRA. They give you the opportunity to benefit from appreciation in the stock price of the company, in addition to providing current income. For example, you might have a $1,000 bond of Bubbles Beverage Company, which pays 7 percent interest annually *and* is convertible into 50 shares of the company's common stock at $20 per share. Until the bond matures, Bubbles Beverage Company promises to pay you $70 per year in two equal payments of $35. At maturity, Bubbles Beverage Company will pay you the $1,000 face amount. You have the right to convert your bond into stock at any time. As long as Bubbles Beverage Company's stock price is well below the $20 exchange price, the bond price will fluctuate based on market interest rates, as any other bond would. If the stock price exceeds the exchange price, the bond price will begin to fluctuate with the stock price. Why? Because if the bond can be exchanged for 50 shares and the stock price is $22 per share, the bond is now worth $1,100 (50 shares times $22). In this way, you can have the stability of a bond with the common stock potential of capital appreciation.

$$Money Mistake: Don't invest your IRA in municipal bonds. Because their interest payments are exempt from federal (and in some cases state and local) taxes, they pay lower interest rates. Since your IRA will defer taxes, don't accept a lower rate to obtain the tax exemption.

Another type of bond often considered for retirement accounts is the *zero-coupon bond*. This is simply a U.S. government bond without the interest payments. Who wants a bond that doesn't pay interest? You might, if you knew that you could buy it for much less than its face value ($1,000) and receive $1,000 when it matures. In effect, you receive all the interest due at maturity. While this is not the growth investment we usually recommend for IRAs, it has two benefits. One is the ability to predict exactly how much money you will have available on a certain date. While we hope that the value of our stocks and mutual funds will grow at a nice rate, there is no guarantee. On the other hand, when you purchase a zero-coupon bond, you can be sure that exactly $1,000 will mature on July 1, 2010. The second benefit is the fact that you can purchase such a bond with a small amount of money. For example, in September of 1994 you could have purchased a bond for $300 that would mature for $1,000 in November of 2009. The implied annual rate of return was about 8.1 percent. This makes it easy to plan for specific occasions such as the first year of retirement.

If you have invested the maximum in both your 401(k) and IRA, what is next? There are two more ways to invest, which delay current income taxes on dividends, interest, and capital gains: annuities and cash-value life insurance. Both are sold by insurance companies.

Annuities

While the amount invested in an annuity is not tax-deductible, annuities offer tax-deferral on investment income and capital gains until the money is withdrawn. Just as with an IRA or 401(k) plan, there are penalties for withdrawing your money from an annuity before you reach the age of 59½. Whenever you withdraw the funds, current income taxes are due on the amount in excess of what you originally invested. For example, just as with a nondeductible IRA, if you invest $2,000 and your account is worth $3,000 when you withdraw it, you owe income taxes on the difference, or $1,000.

As we discussed in Chapter 5, annuities come in two forms: variable and fixed. A variable annuity is simply a managed fund (similar to a mutual fund) of investments wrapped in a tax-deferred package. Its returns are not guaranteed, but will fluctuate with the performance of the underlying investments. One insurance company may offer many variable annuities, which have different investment objectives, much the same as multiple funds within one mutual fund family.

A fixed annuity is similar to a bond within a tax-deferred vehicle. The insurance company will generally guarantee fixed annuity holders a particular rate for a certain time period; for example, 6 percent for two years. At the end of the time period, the rate will adjust to current market rates before becoming fixed for another year or two.

Because the benefit of tax-deferral is most effective with growth investments, consider variable, not fixed, accounts if you invest your retirement funds in annuities.

401(k) Tip: An annuity is only as good as the insurance company behind it. Check with A.M. Best or Standard & Poor's for the company's strength rating. Accept nothing less than an "A" rating, and check it periodically.

Disadvantages of annuities

There are several disadvantages to annuities, which you must weigh against the tax advantage to decide if they are a good investment for you.

1) Lack of liquidity: Once you have invested the maximum that you can in 401(k) plans and IRAs, you have a significant amount of your savings in investments that will not be liquid until you reach 59½. Do not put funds into annuities if you believe that you may need to dip into them for college educations or emergencies. In addition to the lack of liquidity created by law, many annuities have high surrender charges, which are effective for six or eight years.

2) Investment performance: Historically, most variable annuities have underperformed their mutual fund counterparts. If you invest in a variable annuity, compare its one-, three-, five-, and 10-year total returns with those of a similar mutual fund. If the annuity returns are significantly lower, you may be better off with a taxable investment that has better performance.

3) High fees: Annuities and insurance products have some of the highest fees in the investment world. You may not see them in the form of commissions, but they can affect your investment in higher fund expenses or surrender charges.

$$ Money Mistake: Ed bought a variable annuity and, after the fact, he did some research that showed the performance of the annuity was well below comparable mutual funds and the S&P 500 for a similar time period. There was no upfront commission—why did his investment salesperson recommend this investment?

While you may not see an initial commission on your investment, annuities and other insurance products have some of the highest commissions paid to the investment salesperson. If the money to pay a high sales commission doesn't come from your initial investment, where does it come from? Either from high surrender fees or from high operating costs, which reduce your investment's total return. Always ask an investment salesperson how much money he or she will make from your investment purchase.

Cash-Value Life Insurance

Many life insurance products promise to build cash value in addition to providing life insurance. While you may hear them called by many names, such as universal life, whole life, or variable life, we call them *cash-value policies* because the potential to build cash value is their common, distinguishing feature.

A cash-value life insurance policy is really two things: life insurance and an annuity packaged together. A portion of each premium pays for your insurance and a portion goes into an investment account, which grows, tax-deferred, until you withdraw it.

The advantages to investing in a cash-value life insurance policy are tax-deferral and the regular manner in which you pay your life insurance bill. Paying a monthly life insurance premium may be a good form of discipline for the investor who finds it hard to save regularly. If you do not have difficulty saving on your own, the benefits of cash-value life insurance are probably outweighed by high fees and relatively low returns on your investment dollars. In general, you will be better off buying less expensive term insurance and investing the difference separately. According to a *Forbes* magazine article (July 18,1994, p. 122) about variable life insurance, "In the worst cases, you end up paying 10 fees: a premium processing charge, a premium tax, an upfront sales commission, a fee to cover your medical exam, a monthly administrative charge, a monthly insurance charge, a 'guaranteed death benefit' charge, an investment advisery fee, a fund overhead fee, and a 'mortality and expense risk' charge. And if you try to escape within the first 10 years or so, you will almost certainly be assessed a surrender charge."

If you are considering a cash-value life insurance policy, ask the following:

1. What are the one-, five-, and 10-year total returns (actual, not projected) on current policies?

2. What are the annual fees on the policy, in both percentage and actual dollar figures?

3. How difficult is it to liquidate the policy?

4. Are there any surrender charges if I do liquidate?

5. How much does the salesperson make on my buying and holding the investment?

Having the answers to these questions now could definitely save you time and money later.

Should you invest your IRA in an annuity?

No. In order to receive the tax-deferral that annuities offer, you must be willing to pay the high fees generally associated with annuities. However, IRA funds already enjoy tax-deferral; so there is no need to pay high fees in order to benefit from tax-deferral. You can probably find a mutual fund with better performance and/or lower fees than an annuity for your IRA account.

Summary

Now Nancy and Jeff should have a clearer understanding how to invest for their retirement. Nancy is part of a growing company and has decided to take advantage of her maximum 10 percent deduction and company matching.

She will invest 50 percent in company stock, 25 percent in a growth stock mutual fund, and 25 percent in a bond fund. Jeff's company is changing from mostly insurance products to a popular, no-load mutual fund family. He feels confident that he can now make good choices and take advantage of his maximum deduction, also. In addition to their 401(k) plans, each has opened an IRA with a mutual fund company and plans to add to it periodically during the year. Through advance planning and monthly savings, they can make the most of the tax breaks available for retirement saving.

Chapter Eight

Is Your Money Safe? (Or Don't Let Your Nest Egg Crack)

You have determined where you are, know where you are going, and know how to get there. You have taken the time to wisely choose each investment; you know how to analyze and compare total returns. But have you stopped to ask yourself, "Is my retirement money at risk?" Are you sure your savings are safe? If you don't make an annual review of your 401(k) plan, how can you be sure? Chances are your plan is in good shape, but if you file away those boring statements and prospectuses without even a glance, or worse yet, throw them away, you may be costing yourself money. This chapter is dedicated to helping you review and understand *everything* about your plan. You will learn the questions to ask to insure you get the answers you need. These questions won't change from year to year, but the answers sure can. Use this chapter as your framework to make sure your financial foundation is solid, not full of cracks.

It's true that the retirement focus *is* shifting from employers making choices (defined benefit/pension plans) to employees making choices (defined contribution plans). You are now the manager of your money, and it is your responsibility to periodically check out the plan's administrators, performance, and fees to make sure your money is safe. You may think, "Isn't that why we pay the manager?

Why is it so important for *me* to check out my plan? I work hard and don't really have time for this." Defined contribution plans such as 401(k)s and 403(b)s are unlike defined benefit/pension plans. Your net benefit depends on the performance of your investment choices. If you do not choose your investments skillfully, you could have a smaller retirement check than you expected. Statistics show that after approximately 30 years on the job, the average pension plan pays around 35 percent of your final salary. In contrast, how much you receive investing in a 401(k) plan depends basically on you and a few "hows":

◆ How much you set aside pre-tax

◆ How wisely you manage the account

◆ How much the company matches

◆ How well the investments within the plan perform

◆ How the stock and bond markets perform over time

◆ How interest rates rise or fall

◆ How much inflation goes up or down

As you can see, many of these "hows" are unknowns and out of your immediate control. What, then, can you do to make sure your dollars for the future will be there when you need them? First of all, let's go back to the beginning. You need to understand exactly how your plan works and be familiar with each investment option available. If you still don't fully understand your plan or it has been changed, get your hands on all the new information as soon as possible. It has probably come in the mail or across your desk in the past, but may not have been a priority. Now it is! Block off a few hours and thoroughly read your plan documents. Yes, they are a bit technical and a bit boring, but the point is to make sure the people in charge are doing what you expect and that your choices are performing suitably. We suggest you take notes and write down questions along the way to get the very most out of your time and money. Going through this procedure is the only way you will know if your nest egg is safe.

401(k) Tip: A time of crisis is *not* the time to inquire into your plan's safety. It only takes a couple of hours, and is well worth the time spent, to do it *now*.

Questions for Your Plan Check-up

1) Who is in charge of the plan? Is it a mutual fund company, bank, brokerage firm, trust, or insurance company? While it is true that you are in charge of your investment choices, you are not in control of the plan as a whole. Knowing more about the trustee or manager and how he or she works is the first step to establishing a higher "safety" factor in your mind. Once you have a little information on their background, history, and track record, you will have a benchmark for future reference.

2) What is their history? How long have they been in business? Finding out the answer to these questions entails a background search through your human resource department or your corporate or local library. You can use the S&P Reports or S&P Corporate Records to search for more information about the administrator's stability. You are looking for a strong, healthy trustee or administrators with an S&P rating of A, A+, or A++. Remember, their financial stability can directly affect yours.

3) If any of your investment options are GICs (guaranteed investment contracts) or annuities, how stable is the insurance company backing the funds? What is its A.M. Best rating? This is very important to check annually because a very high percentage of 401(k) and 403(b) dollars is invested in GICs and annuities every year. Don't just assume that because the rate is fixed like a CD, a GIC is as safe as a CD. They are similar, as GICs are designed to provide investors with a fixed yield for a fixed time period, usually one to five years, but what isn't so similar is the fact that a bank CD is backed by assets of the bank as well as FDIC insurance. Remember, both GICs and annuities are issued by insurance companies, so the stability and security of your investment is only as secure as the insurance company itself.

The first thing you can do is find out from your local library if the A.M. Best rating has changed over the past year. Just like a test score in school, A+ is the best and can give you an indication of the financial stability of the insurance company. If the rating drops to a B- or C from an A+ over the period of a year, it may be a "red flag" telling you to switch out of this fund. As you investigate your GICs and annuities, you will find out what the insurance company invests in and how they make money with your money. If their investments meet your approval, great! If not, you may want to avoid the GIC option in your plan and bring this information to the attention of your benefits director. The good news is that, to date, none of the insurers that offer contracts have defaulted on their GIC obligations. But there is always risk of the insurers loading their portfolios with bad investments, such as risky mortgages or junk bonds.

401(k) Dilemma: Mark checked his GIC account's latest rating and found one company had changed from an A+ to a B- rating. Upon further review through corporate records, he discovered Star Insurance Company had invested heavily in junk bonds and real estate limited partnerships gone bad. What should Mark do? He has 25 percent of his 401(k) invested in the GIC option and is concerned that this insurance company will go into default.

He should find out whether his GIC is made up of many insurance company contracts or just one. If there are contracts from many companies, his risk is not as great but he should continue to check on a regular basis and be able to move quickly to an account with a similar investment objective if necessary. If Star Insurance Company is the only company in the GIC or is a single investment outside his 401(k), he should definitely take action. Depending on individual state statutes, if the company were to become insolvent, the state's insurance guarantee fund might cover some of Mark's loss. However, it is possible that some states would not cover his GIC, and he could end up losing his entire investment. Checking the rating once per year could save him from an unfortunate situation.

4) What's the load or cost of my 401(k) or 403(b)? Keeping in mind that there is no "free" lunch in the investment world, it is helpful to know the costs and understand where they come from. They usually break down into three different types.

First, there are basic bookkeeping costs (also known as administrative fees), which depend mainly on the plan size. They could range from $25 per employee for a plan with 5,000 participants to a much higher $100 per employee for smaller plans of 100 participants or less. Included in this figure are general overhead and management fees such as utilities, phone service, and mailing costs.

Second, there are asset management fees, which change depending on the maintenance of the individual investment choices and their corresponding managers. For example, each mutual fund option within your plan may have a separate manager, and the stock growth fund may have a different management fee than the bond fund. What should you be paying? A normal range is .50 percent for a bond fund, .75–1.00 percent for a stock fund, and 1.50–1.75 percent for an international stock fund. A bond fund does not require as much management as a stock fund, hence the lower fee. Since an international fund may incur higher expenses due to trading on foreign stock exchanges, their fees are normally higher.

Lastly, you could incur a one-time sales charge or commission on your mutual fund options within your 401(k) plan. A *front-end load* or sales charge is a commission charged as a percentage of the total amount initially invested. By law, the rate cannot exceed 8.5 percent, and there is typically a sliding scale so that larger investments are charged a lower percent in commission. When you invest large amounts (generally outside your 401(k)plan), you may pay a lower commission. Investing enough to qualify for the lower rate is referred to as hitting a *breakpoint*. For example, a fund may charge 4 percent on the first $50,000 you invest, but reduce the charge down to 3 percent once you invest $50,000–$100,000 or more.

Another sales charge you may incur is a *back-end load*, also known as a *contingent deferred sales charge*. This is simply a fancy way of saying the load or commission on the investment is paid when the shares are sold. It is computed as a percentage of the net asset value (NAV) at the time of redemption. For example, if you are selling shares of a fund worth $10,000 and there is a back-end load of 3 percent, you will pay $300.00 ($10,000 times 3 percent). Let's say when you opened the fund three years ago, you started with an investment of $8,000. If you had paid a front-end load of 3 percent at the beginning, you would have paid only $240. Of course, you would pay less if the fund value dropped below the beginning balance of $8,000, and that is a lose-lose situation.

401(k) Tip: Always know what it takes to get out of an investment before you get in.

Many funds have a declining fee scale, which rewards the investor for owning the shares for a longer period of time. For example, the fee in the first year to sell your shares might be 6 percent, in the second year 5 percent, and so on. Many annuities are set up with *back-end loads* using the declining fee scale, which often starts at 8 percent in the first year and declines slowly to 0 percent over a period of nine years. These fees can restrict your ability to make changes in your investment objectives or to move out of investments that are not performing well.

$$ Money Mistake: Be careful when you switch annuity assets into another investment choice (i.e., a fixed annuity to a variable annuity) within the same insurance company. You may start the back-end load schedule all over again. For example, if you owned the original product for five or six years and were down to a redemption fee of only 2 or 3 percent, then switched, you might be locked into an 8 percent fee all over again.

If your plan uses no-load mutual funds, you don't have to worry about commissions, as there is no fee to invest or to liquidate your investment.

5) What percentage of all fees is paid annually by your employer? In the past, employers have paid for record-keeping and basic administrative costs, while the employee pays for asset management. However, the days of the employer picking up the entire tab for your retirement expenses are disappearing quickly.

Can these fees change? It is up to the trustee of the plan to decide how and in what amount to raise fees. The larger your company, the more leverage it will have with the trustee to keep fees reasonable. We recommend looking at your plan's literature annually so that you know what fees are charged.

6) Are there any "hidden" fees? Another charge applied by many mutual funds within a 401(k) plan is called a *12(b)-1 fee*. These fees, which are deducted annually from the total value of your account, are generally computed as a percent of net asset value and are paid to the broker of record. Fees of 0.25 percent to 0.35 percent, annually, are reasonable, but beware of so-called no-load funds, which advertise no upfront charges, but have an excessive 12b-1 of 1 percent or more annually.

$$ Note: In *Morningstar Mutual Funds,* 12b-1 fees are included in the expense ratio and because of this, total returns also reflect their deduction. The *Morningstar* code for a 12b-1 fee is **B**.

401(k) Dilemma: June invests $1,000 per year for 25 years in her 401(k) plan and earns an annual average total return of 9 percent. She should accumulate $78,668 assuming she only pays 0.5 percent in yearly fees. What if she had to pay three times that in fees, or 1.5 percent? Using the same assumptions as above, June would end up with $67,978 or $10,690 (14 percent) less for the extra 1 percent. Ouch!! Know what you pay! The main message is to be aware of the fees you are paying and fully understand the ramifications to your account's bottom line.

Keep asking questions to find out exactly how your individual plan works and what fees apply. You may not be able to change the rules single-handedly, but if your voice joins many, it will be heard. Making your employers know how you feel about high fees should put the pressure on providers. If you aren't aware, you can't make changes.

What Are My Rights under ERISA?

You are entitled to certain rights under the Employee Retirement Income Security Act of 1974 (ERISA), such as:

◆ You can examine, without charge and at the plan administrator's office, all documents filed with the U.S. Department of Labor. This includes detailed annual reports and plan descriptions. Even though you can find detailed data about your plan administrators, they are required to keep all information regarding your account confidential unless your permission is given or those records are subpoenaed by a court of law.

◆ You can obtain copies of all documents and other plan information upon written request to the plan administrator. The administrator may make a reasonable charge for the copies.

◆ You are entitled by law to receive a summary of the plan's annual financial report from the plan administrator.

◆ You can obtain a statement telling you what your benefit would be if you stopped working under the plan now. If you are not yet vested, the statement will tell you how many more years you have to work to be vested. This statement must be requested in writing and is not required to be given more than once per year. It must be provided free of charge.

◆ If you requested materials and did not receive them within 30 days, you may file suit in a federal court.

◆ Your employer cannot fire you to prevent you from receiving a benefit or exercising your rights under ERISA.

The people who operate your plan are called fiduciaries and have the duty to operate it prudently and in the best interest of you and other participants or beneficiaries. If you have any questions, you should contact the nearest Area Office of the U.S. Labor-Management Services Administration, Department of Labor.

Dangerous Pitfalls

On average, 401(k)s have lower total returns than pension plans. Why? The difference is due to the fact that many 401(k) and 403(b) investors are inexperienced money managers. They are not as knowledgeable as pension professionals in making good financial decisions. Lack of education and investment experience often sends 401(k) investors down the conservative path for fear of the risks in alternative choices. There is nothing wrong with being a conservative investor, but don't be one simply because you do not understand other investment options. In this case, being safe can make you sorry. According to Access Research, in 1993, 27 percent of 401(k) assets were held in GICs, mainly due to the promised fixed level of return and the feeling of safety. Only 16 percent of 401(k) money is invested in diversified stocks, which beat the 7.7 percent return of GICs by returning around 10 percent annually since 1926. Pension managers have a mere 2 percent of their assets in GICs and 54 percent in stocks, so it is no wonder their returns are higher than most 401(k)s.

Department of Labor's Rule 404(c)

You may feel like the deck is stacked against you when it comes to managing money, but there is hope. While much of the responsibility in 401(k) investing is on the employee, many employers are complying with Department of Labor rules and regulations regarding 401(k)s. The Department of Labor has issued a voluntary guideline in section 404(c) of ERISA, which recommends that employers do the following:

◆ Offer at least three diversified investment options with different levels of risk within a 401(k) plan (company-stock purchase plans and GICs do not qualify as diversified).

◆ Allow employees to move money from one investment to another at least once every three months and
at any time during the quarter, not just on a specified
day.

◆ Provide prospectuses and education about each investment option.

◆ Provide education on investing principles as well as
information on each of the choices offered by the plan.

◆ Re-educate employees if conditions within the plan
change.

Summary

You don't have to be a financial genius to decipher the
basic information of your plan's reports—just an inter-
ested individual who wants to make the most of each investment. You wouldn't expect a house to be
maintenance-free, so don't think your retirement account
can go without annual repairs, either. Apply due dili-
gence; make sure things are safe before you have a problem that can't be repaired. You *should have* questions for
your benefits administrator or human resource department, that's the only way you can obtain data for financial
decisions. It is much better to ask, than to contribute for 20
or 30 years without making sure your money is safe. It is
an employer's responsibility to provide you with information and answer your questions—but it is up to *you* to ask
the questions.

Chapter Nine

Leaving the Company—
Retiring or Not

If you plan on leaving your company, for whatever reason, be sure to exit with caution. Whether it is due to a job change, termination, or retirement, you will be faced with several major decisions. If you have carefully saved for retirement, you could receive a very large sum of money, which could be the primary source of your future financial security. With that in mind, you can appreciate the importance of maintaining it as a retirement fund rather than considering it "found money," ready for spending. The statistics showing how many people simply spend what took years to save are astounding. Don't be among them!

401(k) Plan Distribution Options

You have several options when leaving your present company. While we can't tell you what to do, we can tell you what *not* to do. If at all possible, avoid taking either of the first two options that follow. They will cost you money.

Don't: Take your distribution in cash, spend it, or deposit it into an account that is not tax-protected

If you take the distribution in cash from your 401(k) account, the amount of the distribution will be added to your current income when computing the income taxes that you owe for the year. You will be responsible for income taxes on everything except after-tax contributions, and you will be charged an additional 10 percent early withdrawal penalty by the IRS unless:

◆ You are under age 55 and "separated from service" or leaving your job.

◆ You are over age 59½.

◆ You are totally and permanently disabled as defined by your plan.

◆ You have a catastrophic medical need.

◆ You've selected to take the distribution in the form of annuitized payments.

If Uncle Sam's threats of taxes and penalties don't deter you from "impulse" spending your retirement fund, maybe an example on the power of compounding can convince you—see the following 401(k) Dilemma.

401(k) Dilemma: Let's say that you are transferring to a new company and have just received a lump-sum check for $15,000. You have been dying for a new car. Should you incur the penalties and pay the taxes to spend the money now, or continue saving the money for later? Hmmm... your impulses want immediate gratification, but your conscience is pleading, "save, save, save." How can you decide?

401(k) Solution: Anytime you are dealing with money, simply run the numbers and let them speak for themselves. If you are 35 and plan to retire at age 65, $15,000 could grow to $261,741 by retirement, based on an average rate of total return of 10 percent. Now, is that new dream car worth $261,741? Probably not. *Save*, rather than *spend*, your rollover.

Spending is tempting until you see the difference in black and white. Keeping the money invested for retirement may be a difficult decision, but the numbers can convince you.

If you are over 59½ and are retiring, you probably won't need all the money at once. By keeping it in a tax-protected account, such as an IRA, you can withdraw as much as you need each year, thereby delaying income taxes on the amount held in the IRA for as long as possible.

Don't: Take your distribution as a rollover

To complete a rollover, you have 60 days from the date you receive your distribution to "roll it over" into a tax-deferred account such as an IRA or the 401(k) plan of a new employer. If you complete the rollover within the designated time frame you will not be responsible for current income taxes (or any penalty if you are under 59½) on the distribution. This was a very popular method of taking 401(k) account distributions until January of 1993.

As of January 1, 1993, federal income tax law regulating rollovers requires that employers who make 401(k) or 403(b) distributions to employees withhold 20 percent of the value of the account and remit it to the IRS as a potential tax payment. (You can get a refund of the withholding if you roll over, but not until tax refund time.)

If you do receive a distribution and elect to roll it over within 60 days, you have to come up with the missing 20 percent. If you do not, and you roll only the 80 percent you received, the missing 20 percent will be taxed and penalized as an early distribution. If you come up with the 20 percent from other sources, you will get that money back when you file for a refund.

401(k) Dilemma: Susan is 48, has left her job, and has $40,000 in her company 401(k) plan. She hadn't decided how to invest the money, and thus didn't give her former employer instructions for a transfer of the funds. One day she received a check in the mail. The check was for $32,000, which was the $40,000 value of the account less 20 percent withholding that had been sent directly to the IRS. To avoid taxes and penalties, she must roll over $40,000 (making up the $8,000 difference herself) into an IRA within 60 days. Then she can file to get the $8,000 back next April. If she only deposits the $32,000 into the IRA, she'll owe a 10 percent penalty plus current income taxes on the $8,000.

In order to avoid this potential headache, have your distribution sent directly from the old custodian to the new custodian in what is called a *transfer*, not a rollover.

Do: Transfer the funds to a self-directed IRA or other tax-deferred plan

The easiest way to maintain the tax-protected status of your 401(k) distribution is to transfer it into an IRA or the 401(k) or 403(b) plan of a new employer.

401(k) Tip: There are no limits to the amount you can transfer into an IRA if the money is coming from a qualified 401(k) plan. There are also no limits to the number of transfers that you may have in any one year.

Once you have chosen a destination for your distribution, whether it is the 401(k) or 403(b) plan of a new employer or an IRA with a bank, brokerage firm, or mutual fund company, communicate this in writing to the administrator of your current plan. Include in your letter:

◆ Your 401(k) or 403(b) account number

◆ Your Social Security number

◆ A copy of your last statement

◆ The date of your employment change

◆ Pertinent information about the new custodian

Be sure to include the new custodian's address and any transfer papers that the current administrator will need. It may be wise to include a reminder with the request stating that the transfer is a *direct* transfer, not a rollover. By completing your request in writing, you have a record of what was sent and when, not just a name on the other end of the phone line.

While most transfers are completed custodian-to-custodian, without your ever having to handle a check, some custodians will mail the check to you, made out to your new custodian. Do not panic. Unless the check is made out to you, it is still a transfer, not a rollover. It should read, "Money Center Bank, custodian for the IRA of Jack Watkins." You should then send it on to your new custodian.

$$ Money Mistake: When Cheryl left her employer, she promptly completed the paperwork for a transfer of her 401(k) distribution. One month later, she received a check (made out to her) in the mail from her employer. Realizing that they had made a mistake in sending the check to her, but not paying much attention to the amount of the check, she simply endorsed it and sent it to her new custodian.

What should she have done? She should have sent it back to her employer with a copy of her letter of instruction, directing them to issue another check, made out to her new custodian without withholding 20 percent.

You do not have to choose how to invest your distribution when you make the transfer, only who will be the custodian. For example, if you like the Fidelity family of mutual funds, but are unsure of which specific funds you want to invest in, or perhaps are concerned about the state of the stock market, you can transfer to an IRA at Fidelity and keep your money in a money market account until you make a decision. Don't let the prospect of designating a new custodian hurry you into making an investment decision. If you are not sure about a mutual fund company, open a self-directed IRA with a bank or brokerage firm and deposit the money into their money market fund. Later, you can purchase stocks, bonds, or mutual funds as you choose.

If you are transferring your distribution into an existing IRA, make sure that you understand the consequences of *co-mingling*. While it is perfectly legal to take your distribution and combine it with an existing IRA, you will lose the ability to transfer your distribution into an employer's plan in the future if you co-mingle your distribution with ordinary IRA funds.

If you have a waiting period to get into a new employer's plan and are not comfortable leaving your retirement funds with your old employer, direct the old custodian to transfer the proceeds into a self-directed IRA to hold your money until you can transfer it to the new 401(k). Keep the money separate from any other IRA funds that you may already have. The best way to assure this is to open an account at an institution where you do not have other funds to avoid co-mingling by mistake.

401(k) Dilemma: Grant is receiving a lump-sum distribution and already has an IRA to which he has been contributing $2,000 per year for the past four years. He is inbetween jobs and needs a place to park the distribution until he gets another job. Should he add this lump sum to his existing IRA to save paperwork?

401(k) Solution: If he is planning to get another job in the near future, he should open a new IRA for the distribution. Then, if he has the option of transferring the distribution into his new employer's plan and decides that he likes the plan investments and their performance, he can transfer the money into his new employer's

401(k) plan. If he mixes even one dollar of the distribution with his existing IRA, he cannot reverse the process.

If Grant goes to work for a company that does not offer a 401(k) plan, he still may want to have the money segregated for other reasons. One would be the possibility of starting his own company and setting up his own qualified retirement plan. You may not mind mixing the retirement funds if you would rather manage them yourself, using any of the vast array of investment options available on the market. If you are in retirement and will not be moving on to another employer, there is no reason to keep separate IRAs. Having only one account to manage, and only one trustee fee to pay, may make the most sense in this case.

401(k) Dilemma: Cindy is leaving her company and hasn't had time to completely research a new custodian for the distribution from her former employer's 401(k) plan. She knows she wants a mutual fund family with a money market fund, growth stock fund, bond fund, and international aggressive fund, but isn't sure how much of the proceeds to allocate to each choice. What should she do?

401(k) Solution: Cindy should transfer the money into an interest-bearing account (i.e., money market) at the fund while analyzing the other fund family choices. After she picks a suitable investment(s), she can move the money from the money market to the funds of her choice. This will alleviate some of the initial pressure and give her time to make wise investment moves at her own pace.

Leave the funds in your
former employer's plan

In many cases you may be encouraged to take your distribution to cut back on administrative costs within the plan. However, you may have the right to leave it in the plan. It is important to find out the individual company's rules governing this situation and know all of your choices. Obviously, you will not continue to receive company matching, and you must consider whether this is the best place to leave your money. Are you happy with the performance of the investment options offered, or do you think you might be able to do better on your own? Investigate and decide which is better for you and your money. If you do leave the money there, periodically check your investments to make sure they are meeting your expectations.

Have the old employer transfer the funds to
your new employer's 401(k) or 403(b) plan

If you already have a new job and there is not a waiting period to enroll in your new employer's 401(k) or 403(b) plan, you may want to have your distribution transferred directly to it. Some employers will accept rollovers from another employer, but will not accept direct transfers. Check to see what yours will allow. You may need to transfer into an IRA temporarily, then perform a rollover into the new plan. This will allow you to avoid the 20 percent withholding, as it does not apply to rollovers that come from IRAs, only those that come from employer plans.

Take your distribution in the form of company stock

You don't have to sell the company stock in your 401(k) plan just because you are retiring or leaving the company. If you are retiring, have other investments in different levels of your personal pyramid, and believe that your company stock is a good, long-term holding, consider taking your distribution in stock and keeping it. Make sure that your investments are not so concentrated in the stock that any volatility in the price would threaten your retirement. (Remember when IBM was over $100 a share?) If you are not retiring and consider the stock a good investment, transfer it to a self-directed IRA. In an exception to the 20 percent rollover withholding rule, distributions that are entirely employer contributions of the employer's company stock are excluded from withholding. In this case, it is as convenient to do a rollover as a direct transfer. Remember, the downside to having your retirement totally in your former company's stock is that you are taking a big risk by having so many of your eggs in one basket.

Plan, don't panic

Don't panic just yet. If you are leaving your employer and have a 401(k) or 403(b) plan, do the following:

◆ Get a distribution form and all information about your current plan.

◆ Find out the market value of your account and exactly how much you will be receiving, when.

◆ If you have a new employer, check to see if they have a 401(k) or 403(b) and if you can transfer funds into their plan.

◆ Investigate your current plan to see if you can leave your savings in the plan and, if so, for how long.

◆ Learn about self-directed IRA accounts offered by your local banks and brokerage firms.

◆ Avoid rollovers and the automatic 20 percent withholding by using a direct transfer.

Once the money is safely transferred into a new account, all the old rules still apply. After age 59½ and up to age 70½, you may withdraw any amount without penalty. Once you reach age 70½, you are obligated to begin some sort of withdrawal process and will be taxed accordingly.

401(k) Tip: You don't know how long you will be around after retirement, so don't take the chance of outliving your assets. You want your money to keep working even after you quit.

Early retirement ... Company choice

Over the past few years, thousands of workers have been given the opportunity to trade in their jobs to pursue other interests in exchange for a cash settlement. If this has happened to you, you may be asking yourself, "Should I stay or should I go?" It is a tough decision that usually needs to be made rather quickly, often within 90 days. There will most likely be company meetings to discuss the available options and documents describing the plan, but the first thing to do is understand what type of offer you are facing. The two main types are early retirement programs and voluntary separation packages.

Early retirement programs:

- ◆ The most common packages offered by employers
- ◆ Offer benefits only to employees nearing retirement age
- ◆ Are not negotiable by law

Voluntary separation packages:

- ◆ Can offer benefits to any employee
- ◆ Are negotiable

$$ Money Mistake: Nancy was offered an early retirement package at IBG, which provided a bonus of $10,000, two year's pay, and 18 months of paid medical benefits. She wasn't sure she was ready to retire and thought, "Why not hold out just a little longer for a better deal?" One year later plans were announced to totally shut down the plant. Now, the offer she can't refuse amounts to only one year's pay and no medical benefits. Make sure you carefully consider the benefits offered in early retirement options, especially if your company is having financial difficulties.

The main thing to consider in early retirement, whether it is your choice or your company's, is timing. Ask yourself a few questions:

- ◆ Can you afford to retire now, and do you want to?

◆ Is it time to make a career change?

◆ Is it time to go back to school for more education?

Only you have the answers. Early retirement in the 1990s has forced many employees to suddenly switch roles and become their own employers. Thousands of small businesses have been created by people who would never have had the capital or the guts to go it on their own. It is not all bad to be forced into taking a long, hard look at your "job" life. You may or may not like what is staring back at you, but after you have come to grips with your emotions, it is easier to be objective and evaluate the offer.

Moving on: Getting the best offer

How can you tell if your offer is good? Here are some benchmarks:

1) First of all, the best packages will offer you two to three weeks of salary for every year you have worked. Many companies have been known to add five years to your age and to the time you have worked for them, for the purpose of deciding your pension benefits. (This is the only time you want to gain five years overnight!) This can certainly enhance your pension and substantially sweeten the pot.

2) The other very important, but sometimes overlooked, issue on the buyout offer is health insurance. Price insurance for an individual in the open market if you think this issue is insignificant. Health insurance is a huge benefit we sometimes take for granted each day we walk through the company door. Early retirement plans are offered most often to employees age 50 or older, and the best plans continue to offer health insurance until normal retirement age. This is a considerable figure to take into account.

If you are far from retirement age, you may be offered a voluntary separation package. There are innumerable possible scenarios. In many of the best, the company picks up the tab for insurance benefits for 12 to 18 months. Some may even share the cost with the employee for an extended period of time. This may allow you to secure another position without feeling under so much pressure to accept the first job that comes along.

Early retirement ... Your choice

If you are satisfied with your job, but are simply trying to calculate how you can retire from the rat race sooner, here are some tips.

1) Live on less now to have more later. This *is* possible, even if there doesn't seem to be enough money left at the end of the month the way it is. It may be easier than it sounds: just think of every outlay of money you make as future interest. For example, for every thousand dollars you spend, you are choosing to give up $100 in interest every year for the rest of your life, assuming you could earn an average of 10 percent over a lifetime. It sure takes the fun out of shopping trips and may curtail a few vacations, but it is a reality check if you really want to retire sooner. How can you do it? Living on less now could mean buying a used car instead of a new one or living in a smaller house outside of the city or in a less expensive area. Conscious efforts must be applied daily to make living on less a routine. It is truly an art and may take a little practice.

401(k) Tip: Don't pay more than 25 percent of your gross salary in monthly mortgage expense. Your house is a prime candidate for cutbacks, as your mortgage payment can take a big bite out of your budget every month. Since mortgage expense is often the largest monthly expense incurred, reducing it greatly enhances the possibility of saving more for early retirement.

Better than a penny stock or a "get-rich-quick" scheme, a simple way to save money on a new mortgage is to pay down principal early. For example, homeowners with a new $200,000, 30-year mortgage at 10 percent make monthly payments of $1,755. Ouch! Consider the following:

◆ In the first year, 95 percent of their payments go for interest.

◆ In 30 years, they pay $432,000 in interest charges.

If they add just $50 to their monthly payments for the first year *only*, for a total of $600 extra dollars, the mortgage will be paid off six months early, and the total interest charge reduced by $10,434. If they continue the extra payments over the life of the loan, it will be paid off in 26 years and they will save $73,000. What about the interest deduction on their taxes? Because 95 percent of the first year's payments go to pay interest, $600 in extra principal payments reduces the first year's interest deduction of $19,950 by only $28, to $19,922.

401(k) Tip: Save now to spend later. Assuming a $200,000 mortgage for 30 years at 10 percent, if you add $25 to your monthly payment, you can save $41,343 in 30 years. Add $100 and save $120,655. Add $200 and save $181,007 ... that's a lot of money!

2) Work part-time during early retirement. This way you can still be part of the workforce and continue to earn an income while working less. A part-time job could also allow you to receive very important benefits such as health insurance until *real* retirement age hits and Social Security or your pension kick in.

3) Consider moving into a smaller home once your children have left the nest. Many who are nearing retirement take advantage of the gains they have in their homes and invest some of the proceeds into more rapidly growing investments.

401(k) Dilemma: Ruth and Rolf are 50-something and live in a metropolitan area. Their house is valued at $200,000 and they owe a mortgage balance of only $30,000. Should they sell and pocket the difference for early retirement?

401(k) Solution: If they are willing to live in a more modest home (if their children have left home, they probably won't need as much space), they could sell, pay off the old mortgage, buy a new home, and invest the balance for retirement. Using their one-time IRS exemption on the capital gain, they could live comfortably with no mortgage payment and an account that is growing for retirement.

How much will you need to live on if you retire early?

No matter when you retire, you will want to be sure that, given your combined sources of income, you can maintain a comfortable lifestyle. Chapter 6 is devoted to helping you determine just how much you will need. Use the different retirement worksheets and a different number of years until retirement to see how your financial situation will change if you retire early.

$$ Money Mistake: You may be tempted to gather all of your retirement dollars in qualified, tax-deferred accounts such as 401(k) plans and IRAs. Think twice before you do this if your goal is to retire before age 59½. Be sure to invest some of your retirement funds outside such accounts so that you do not incur penalties when withdrawing before age 59½.

Retirement choices: How do you want your money?

Typically, employer retirement plans offer several ways for you to take the balance of your plan account at retirement. The following are some of the options from which you may be able to choose:

Lump-sum payment: You will receive your retirement distribution in the form of one single payment or several payments over a short period of time. After you receive the check, you will have no further rights to the plan, and it becomes your responsibility to invest the proceeds. If you do not need the money immediately and have not yet reached the age of 70½, you can transfer your distribution (excluding after-tax investments) into a self-directed IRA or mutual fund IRA. A lump sum is one of the most common ways that companies distribute benefits, and in the case of very small accounts ($3,500 or less), may be the only option offered.

Life annuity: You will receive a monthly annuity for the rest of your life. After your death, no further payments will be made on your behalf. With a life annuity payment option, your trustee purchases an annuity from an insurance company with the balance of your 401(k) account. The insurance company assumes all risk of investment performance and of your living a very long time.

Life annuity with 10-year term certain: You will also receive a monthly annuity for the rest of your life with this option, but in addition, if you die before the 10 years have passed, remaining payments up until 10 years will be paid to a named beneficiary. If you die after the 10 years have passed, payments cease. Since there is a guarantee of at least 10 years' worth of payments, each payment will generally be lower than those of a life annuity that does not have a "term" feature.

Annuity for 10 years: You will receive an annuity for 10 years under this option. With the term certain, it is possible to outlive the payments. If you die before the 10-year period is expired, the remaining payments will go directly to your named beneficiary. After you or your beneficiary have received payments for 10 years, the payments will stop. This option differs from the one above because you will not continue to receive the annuity for life.

Life annuity with a cash refund feature: This option pays a monthly annuity for life. You will be guaranteed to receive the amount your employer paid to the life insurance company to purchase the annuity. If you die before having received total annuity payments equal to the purchase price, any remaining value will be paid to your named beneficiary. If you die after receiving your guaranteed value, your annuity will work in the same way a life annuity would, by ceasing payments at your death.

Joint and survivor annuity: This annuity is paid until both you and your beneficiary die. No matter who dies first, the survivor continues to receive payments until his or her death, at which time payments cease.

What happens if you die before retirement?

If you die before retirement, your beneficiary is entitled to your 401(k) account balance. No 10 percent penalty is levied, but the recipient will be responsible for the ordinary income taxes. Your beneficiary may be able to choose between a single lump-sum payment or an annuity. If your beneficiary is a surviving spouse, he or she may roll over or transfer the funds into an IRA.

What is spousal consent?

You may name someone other than your spouse to receive the benefit that would be paid upon your death. However, this must be agreed to by your spouse in writing. The consent form must be notarized or witnessed by a plan representative. This form will specifically state what the agreement is. If it is a "general" consent form, you are permitted to change your beneficiary without again obtaining your spouse's permission.

401(k) Dilemma: Paul and his wife, Maureen, have decided to change Paul's beneficiary to their daughter. Maureen has given her general consent to allow this to happen. Later, if Paul decides to change it to their son, he can do this without the consent of Maureen. If you are Maureen, be careful—he can also change the beneficiary to Bambi without your consent.

Your plan may or may not allow you to take back consent once it has been given. Thus, signing such an agreement deserves special thought and should not be taken lightly.

Using forward averaging

If you were born before 1936, are over 59½, and are taking a lump-sum distribution from a 401(k) plan (distributions from tax-sheltered annuities are not eligible), you may take advantage of *five- or 10-year forward averaging.* Although it is called *averaging,* it is simply a special formula used by the IRS to figure the taxes due for the year of receipt. You pay the tax only once, not over the next five or 10 years as the name implies. The tax is in addition to the regular tax figured on your other income. The main advantage is that you may pay less in taxes than you might otherwise.

Who is eligible? To qualify for five- or 10-year forward averaging, you must have been born before 1936, have participated in your company plan for at least 5 years, be 59½ or older at the time you receive the distribution, and have taken your payment in the form of a lump sum. You need to complete IRS Form 4972 and attach it to your Form 1040 return if you choose to use forward averaging.

$$ Note: If you received more than one lump-sum distribution for a plan participant during the year, you must add them together using the special method. Refer to IRS publication 575 for more specific tax information.

Real retirement ... Ready or not!

Don't just stop managing your money because you are retired. We have heard many people claim, "Oh, I don't need to manage my money anymore because I am retired." Not true! Maybe so in the days of the 10 percent and 15 percent certificates of deposit, but not now for Mr. and Mrs. Modern Investor. Not only are CDs yielding much less, demographics show that a man turning 65 can expect to live another 15 years and a woman the same age another 19 years. For these reasons alone, retirement could be the most important stage of your investing career. It is always important to be in control of your finances, but it becomes critical once you enter the non-working population.

401(k) Tip: Your money will not take care of you by itself—you have to give it as much help as possible. You wouldn't expect your automobile to run without regular maintenance, so work hard to keep your retirement account fine-tuned as well.

When do you have to take your money?

Uncle Sam requires you to start annual distributions from your IRA, 401(k) or 403(b) in the year you turn 70½. For example, if your 70th birthday is between January and June, you will be considered 70½ that year and must take a distribution by April 1st of the following year. If you were born between July and December, you won't be considered 70½ until the next year and must take the first withdrawal in the following year.

401(k) Tip: Austin's 70th birthday was April 5th this year. He did not want to take his first year's IRA distribution due to a higher-than-usual income year. He took advantage of the IRS one-year grace period, which allows him to waive the first year's withdrawal until April 1st of the following year. The rule requires he then take two years' worth of withdrawals in the second year. In his case that was fine because he knew he would have considerably less income next year and it would not be a tax burden to take two withdrawals in the same year. However, a "double" distribution could move you into a higher tax bracket and cause Social Security dollars to be exposed to excess taxes as well.

$$ Note: After the first year, withdrawals are due by December 31 of the designated year.

How much money should you take?

Obviously, this is a very personal issue, but we'll explain a few of the formulas used. The IRS required minimum withdrawal is figured using a life expectancy number or the joint life expectancy of you and your named beneficiary. For example, if a 70-year-old has a life expectancy of 16 years and an account balance of $175,000, the first required payout would be 1/16, or 6.25 percent ($10,937.50), of the previous year's ending balance. To go forward, you can either choose to recalculate your life expectancy each year or simply reduce the original number (in this case 16) by one each subsequent year. In other words, 1/15th or 6.66 percent the second year, 1/14th or 7.14 percent the third year, etc. Be careful which method you choose, because once you select a formula, you have to stick to it. See Tables 9-1 or 9-2 for single or joint life expectancy figures.

401(k) Tip: Don't worry about the math. Life expectancy tables can be found in IRS publications 590 and 939. You can call 1-800-829-3676 for a copy or to ask questions. The plan administrator of your accounts should also notify you when it is time to start withdrawals and help figure the minimum requirement.

What should you do if you have more than one retirement account?

Don't panic if you have more than one IRA. You can take the minimum out of any or all of your accounts as long as the total amount withdrawn equals or exceeds the minimum IRS requirement. The tricky part is determining the minimum amount for each account (it gets complicated if you have named different beneficiaries of various ages). However, once you reach a total minimum figure, you can begin withdrawals from the coordinating accounts.

Table 9-1   Single Life Expectancy Table

Age	Life Expectancy		Age	Life Expectancy
65	20		73	13.9
66	19.2		74	13.2
67	18.4		75	12.5
68	17.6		76	11.9
69	16.8		77	11.2
70	16		78	10.6
71	15.3		79	10
72	14.6		80	9.5

Table 9-2   Joint Life and Last Survivor Life Expectancy Table

	Ages	Beneficiary Age									
		60	61	62	63	64	65	66	67	68	69
	65	27.6	27.1	26.5	26.0	25.5	25.0	24.6	24.2	23.8	23.4
	66	27.3	26.7	26.1	25.6	25.1	24.6	24.1	23.7	23.3	22.9
	67	27.0	26.4	25.8	25.2	24.7	24.2	23.7	23.2	22.8	22.4
IRA Owner Age	68	26.7	26.1	25.5	24.9	24.3	23.8	23.3	22.8	22.3	21.9
	69	26.5	25.8	25.2	24.6	24.0	23.4	22.9	22.4	21.9	21.5
	70	26.2	25.6	24.9	24.3	23.7	23.1	22.5	22.0	21.5	21.1
	71	26.0	25.3	24.7	24.0	23.4	22.8	22.2	21.7	21.2	20.7
	72	25.8	25.1	24.4	23.8	23.1	22.5	21.9	21.3	20.8	20.3
	73	25.6	24.9	24.2	23.5	22.9	22.2	21.6	21.0	20.5	20.0
	74	25.5	24.7	24.0	23.3	22.7	22.0	21.4	20.8	20.2	19.6
	75	25.3	24.6	23.8	23.1	22.4	21.8	21.1	20.5	19.9	19.3
	76	25.2	24.4	23.7	23.0	22.3	21.6	20.9	20.3	19.7	19.1
	77	25.1	24.3	23.6	22.8	22.1	21.4	20.7	20.1	19.4	18.8
	78	25.0	24.2	23.4	22.7	21.9	21.2	20.5	19.9	19.2	18.6
	79	24.9	24.1	23.3	22.6	21.8	21.1	20.4	19.7	19.0	18.4
	80	24.8	24.0	23.2	22.4	21.7	21.0	20.2	19.5	18.9	18.2

Tables from IRS Publication 590.

401(k) Tip: If you have several retirement accounts, withdraw funds first from accounts that are earning the lowest returns while letting other accounts accumulate and grow.

What happens if you don't start distributions on time?

Go directly to jail and do not pass GO? Fortunately, that only happens when you play Monopoly, but there are penalties involved if you do not take your distribution on time. It is imperative to understand all of the retirement rules and tax ramifications *before* you reach 70½. Ready or not, Uncle Sam will penalize you 50 percent of the amount you should have removed plus any income taxes that would have been due on the required withdrawal amount. If you do make a mistake, you can request Form #5329 from the IRS, pay the penalties, and attach it to your next year's tax forms.

Summary

I do have time ... I understand my investment options ... I can afford to save now for later ... I know exactly where to start ... I am sure my retirement dollars are safe ... It's easy to analyze a mutual fund ... I'm worrying about retirement today ... No more headaches or hives when it comes to money management ... I can do it!

No more excuses when it comes to money and retirement! You are one of over 16 million people in the United States whose 401(k) investments now total over one-third of a trillion dollars. The Department of Labor's Pension and Welfare Benefits Administration predicts that by the turn of the century these plans will be the backbone of the entire retirement system, climbing to well over 2.8 trillion dollars. Thus, it is vital to participate in this growing trend and take advantage of a retirement savings plan. You have learned that retirement means systematically saving for future needs and accumulating funds to outlive expenses. Since you can't control future expenses, the only controllable issues are saving and investing.

Remember our families from the Introduction? Patty, our single mother, is in the "Getting Growing" stage of life. She has set a short-term goal of building an emergency savings cushion and a long-term goal of saving for her children's college educations and her own retirement. Even though her ex-husband will share college costs, she can no longer count on his company pension. Because she is getting a late start accumulating retirement funds, it is especially important for her to use growth investments. Her investment plan includes:

◆ Building a three- to six-month cash reserve for emergencies

◆ Investing in her 401(k) plan and/or an IRA to create a growth fund for retirement.

Mike and Leslie are nearing the end of the "Getting Growing" stage of life. Their short-term goals are to pay for college educations and to continue to save from current income. Their long-term goal is to accumulate enough savings for retirement. As a dual-income family with children in college, Mike and Leslie are finding it difficult to add to savings due to high current expenses. Their investment plan includes:

◆ Building retirement funds through maximum 401(k) plan contributions (automatic withdrawal will save them from the temptation to spend the money on current expenses)

◆ Paying for college costs with current college savings and using student loans (not retirement savings) for any shortfall

Julie and Marty are in the "Getting Comfortable" stage of life. They have a short-term goal of reducing their tax burden and a long-term goal of establishing a retirement savings fund that will support their current lifestyle. They have about 10 years until retirement, during which they can pad their nest egg. Their investment plan includes:

◆ Maximizing tax deductions and tax deferral through 401(k) contributions

◆ Adding to IRAs, even though the initial contribution is not deductible

These three families can do it, and so can you. You have educated yourself about the basic concepts of successful money management, and you have a plan to get where you want to go. Don't count on someone else to take charge of your financial destiny—it's *your* money!

Appendix A

$$Financial Forms

Use the following forms to detail your plan options and the investment decisions you have made to date. Complete the "401(k) or 403(b) Retirement Plan" each year to document your progress and make sure you are on track to reach your goals.

Table A.1   401(k) or 403(b) Plan Investment Options

Investment Option	Level of Investment Pyramid	Investment Objective	1-Year Total Return	5-Year Total Return	10-Year Total Return
1.					
2.					
3.					
4.					
5.					
6.					

Figure A.2   401(k) or 403(b) Retirement Plan

Date of Eligibility: _____

Date of 1st Contribution: _____

Current Value: $_____

Current Contribution %: _____   Maximum % allowed: _____

Total Contribution Per Year: $_____   Per Paycheck: $_____

How and When to Make Plan Changes: _____

Company Matching %: _____   Per Year: $_____   Per Paycheck: $_____

401(k) Plan	Fund 1	Fund 2	Fund 3	Fund 4
Objective				
% Invested				
Current Value				
Total Return				

Figure A.2   401(k) or 403(b) Retirement Plan (continued)

Are you vested? Yes_____ No_____ When you will be 100% vested?_____

Expected retirement age:_____ Expected value at retirement:_____

Beneficiary(s):_____

Plan Contact Person:_____

Phone:_____

Annual Fee:_____

Termination Fee:_____

Other Terms:_____

Figure A.3   IRA Retirement Plan

Date of 1st Contribution: _____

Current Value: $ _____

Total Contribution Per Year: $ _____

Is it tax deductible? _____

Investment Objective: _____

IRA Plan	Investment A	Investment B	Investment C	Investment D
Objective				
Current Value				
1 Year Total Return				
5 Year Total Return				
10 Year Total Return				

Figure A.3   IRA Retirement Plan (continued)

Expected retirement age: _____

Expected value at retirement: _____

Beneficiary(s): _____

Plan Contact Person: _____

Phone: _____

Annual Fee: _____

Termination Fee: _____

Other Terms: _____

Appendix B

What to Read ...
Where to Find Information

Books

99 Great Answers to Everyone's Investment Questions, the *MONEYWISE* Partners, Linda Bryant, Diane Pearl, and Ellie Williams. You don't have to know all the right answers if you know the right questions. Learn the right questions to ask about investing *and* the answers you should find.

The Smart Woman's Guide to Spending, Saving, and Managing Money, the *MONEYWISE* partners, Ellie Williams Clinton and Diane Pearl. From family budgeting and purchasing cars and homes to investing for college educations, this book covers the practical aspects of managing money. Written for anyone who wants to learn how to make good financial decisions, smart *men* may even want to peek.

One Up On Wall Street, Peter Lynch. A very readable collection of tips, ideas and investing experiences from former Fidelity Magellan manager Peter Lynch. Topics include how to spot growth companies in your every day life and how to create a good investment track record with consistent "singles" and "doubles" instead of the rare "home run."

The Intelligent Investor, Benjamin Graham. An approach to value-based investing from one of the fathers of fundamental analysis.

Liar's Poker, Michael Lewis. An entertaining and sometimes raw recount of a young MBAs rapid rise in Salomon Brother's bond trading department.

The Wall Street Journal Guide to Understanding Money & Markets, Dow Jones. A practical reference guide for a variety of terms, history and examples on how to read financial information from periodicals.

Resources

Most of these should be available at your local library, bank, or from a broker, but prices and subscription information are included for those who would like the convenience of personal copies. Check for low-priced trial subscriptions before you buy.

Value Line Investment Survey is a collection of one-page research reports on over 1,200 different stocks. Each report contains historic and expected financial data plus a ranking (from 1 to 5) of Safety and Timeliness. A one-year subscription costs $525. Call (800) 833-0046.

Value Line Mutual Fund Survey contains one-page research reports on mutual funds. Each report contains past performance figures, current holdings and investment objectives, and an assessment of risk and overall performance. A one-year subscription costs $295. Call (800) 284-7607, extension 6646.

Morningstar Mutual Funds analyzes mutual funds in a one-page format. Besides the historic return and other portfolio information provided, each fund is ranked on a five star system for risk and return performance. A one-year subscription costs $395. Call (800) 876-5005 or (312) 696-6000.

Morningstar Closed-End Funds analyzes closed-end mutual funds. (While open-end funds are purchased and redeemed through the fund company at a price that reflects the underlying value of the portfolio, closed-end funds are traded among investors on a stock exchange and may sell either above or below their portfolio value, based upon supply and demand.) A one-year subscription costs $195. Call (800) 876-5005

Morningstar Variable Annuity/and Life analyzes variable annuities and variable life insurance policies, providing data on past performance and comparisons with peer-groups. A one-year subscription costs $295. Call (800) 876-5005.

Standard & Poor's/Lipper Mutual Fund Profiles contains half-page fund analyses which are updated quarterly. A one-year subscription costs $145. Call (800) 221-5277 or (212) 208-8000.

Glossary

ANNUITY An investment contract sold by a life insurance company which offers tax-deferral on investment growth and income. Annuities can be fixed or variable rate.

AFTER-TAX CONTRIBUTION Contributions to a 401(k) plan which are not deducted from the participant's gross income when computing taxes, but are taxed as any other compensation is. The investment income and growth of these funds do not enjoy the same tax-deferred status as elective contributions, but may be withdrawn without penalty or additional taxes.

BACK-END LOAD A fee paid when an investor sells or redeems shares of a mutual fund or annuity.

BLUE CHIP A company that is known for its ability to make a profit and pay dividends maintaining stock price stability.

BOND Debt of a company, government, or municipality in which the issuer promises to pay the bondholders a specific rate of interest (coupon) until a specified date (maturity). The bondholder is a creditor and not a partial owner as is a stockholder.

BROKER A salesperson who can purchase securities for investors. Brokers are paid by a commission charged with each transaction. Full-service brokers provide advice and recommendations and generally charge higher commissions. Discount brokers provide only the transactional service and usually offer discounted commission. Commission levels can vary widely, even within a service category.

BUSINESS RISK The risk inherent in a company's operations such as the uncertainty about the company sales, profits and rate of return.

CAPITAL GAIN or LOSS Profit or loss from the sale of a capital asset. Under current tax law, capital gains and losses are taxed as ordinary income.

CERTIFICATE OF DEPOSIT A time deposit issued by a bank. It generally has a set maturity date, interest rate, and penalty for early withdrawal.

CHURNING An illegal practice in which unethical securities brokers recommend that their clients buy and sell frequently in order to generate commissions.

CLOSED-END FUND A mutual fund whose shares are traded on a stock exchange, rather than being issued and redeemed by the fund company as in an open-end fund. Share prices are based on supply and demand and may or may not equal the asset value of the shares.

CO-MINGLING Combining funds from an employer retirement account with funds which have been contributed to an ordinary IRA.

COMMON STOCK Securities which represent ownership in a corporation. Their value is based upon supply and demand. They do not have a maturity date and may or may not pay a periodic dividend.

CURRENT YIELD The annual interest or dividend payment as a percentage of the current market price of a security. To compute the current yield divide the annual dividend or interest by the price of the security.

DEFINED BENEFIT PLAN A retirement plan in which the benefit to the employee is stated, such as "50 percent of the employee's final annual salary."

DEFINED CONTRIBUTION PLAN A retirement plan in which contribution amounts (from employee, employer, or both) are stated, but no guarantee of final benefit is made.

DOLLAR COST AVERAGING Investing a regular amount of money at periodic intervals. As a result, the investor buys more of the security when the dollar price is low and less when it rises.

DOW JONES INDUSTRIAL AVERAGE The weighted average of thirty blue chip stocks better known as the DJIA or the "market."

EARNINGS PER SHARE A company's total earnings divided by the number of shares of common stock outstanding. Growth in EPS is a primary factor in analyzing the price potential of its stock.

ELECTIVE CONTRIBUTION The funds which an employee directs his or her employer to withhold from each paycheck and deposit into a 401(k) or 403(b) plan. The employee does not pay current income taxes on elective contributions. When withdrawn, funds are taxed at current income tax rates and, if withdrawn before age 59½, a 10 percent IRS penalty applies.

EQUITY The net worth of a company which consists of capital stock, paid-in capital and retained earnings. Common equity is what belongs to the stockholders.

EX-DIVIDEND (Without dividend) Describes a stock that is trading without the right to its upcoming dividend. When a stock that is trading ex-dividend is sold, the seller is entitled to the dividend and the buyer is not. The ex-dividend date is the first day on which the stock trades without the right to its dividend. It is four business days before the record date.

EXPENSE RATIO The percentage of fund assets paid for operating expenses, management fees, and 12b-1 fees. It does not include sales loads or commissions.

FACE VALUE Also called par value, this is the amount that a company agrees to pay bondholders at maturity. This may or may not be the actual market value of the bond.

FRONT-END LOAD A sales commission paid upon the purchase of a mutual fund. It is generally figured as a percent of the dollars invested.

GUARANTEED INVESTMENT CONTRACT (GIC) A contract issued by an insurance company which promises to pay the investor a specific rate of return for a designated length of time.

GOVERNMENT BONDS Debt of the U.S. Government such as Treasury Bills, Notes and Bonds. Generally regarded as the highest grade bonds in existence.

HARDSHIP DISTRIBUTIONS A distribution which does not meet other plan criteria for a distribution, but is due to the employee's immediate and heavy financial need and is necessary to satisfy that need. Hardship distributions are subject to ordinary income tax and to the 10 percent IRS penalty for withdrawals before age 59½. The following are examples of what is considered immediate and heavy need:

◆ medical expenses previously incurred by the employee, his or her spouse or dependents; amounts necessary for any of these persons to obtain medical care

◆ costs incurred in purchasing a principal residence (this does not include mortgage payments)

◆ tuition and related educational expenses for the next year of post-secondary education for the employee, his or her spouse or dependents

◆ payments to prevent eviction from or foreclosure on a principal residence

LIQUIDITY The characteristic of being readily convertible to cash without suffering a decrease in price if a quick sale must be made.

401(k) PLAN LOANS Many employers allow employees to borrow a portion of their 401(k) account and pay themselves back, with interest. While it is not advisable to use a 401(k) account for current expenses, in the case of financial emergency, it is better to borrow and repay than to withdraw and pay penalties and taxes.

MATCHING At the same time an employee's contribution is deposited, the employer may choose to make a matching deposit in either cash or company stock. Matching is usually expressed as a percent, such as "25 percent matching," which means the employer will deposit $.25 for every $1.00 contributed, up to a specified amount.

MUNICIPAL BOND A bond issued by a state, county, city, or other political subdivision. Generally, interest received on a municipal bond is federally tax exempt and state tax exempt in the issuing state.

NASDAQ Acronym for National Association of Security Dealers Automated Quotations or a nationwide computerized securities market. The NASDAQ market is also known as the "Over the Counter" market.

NET ASSET VALUE (NAV) Used to identify the value of a share of a mutual fund or unit investment trust. The NAV is the total market value of all assets less any liabilities divided by the number of shares outstanding.

PAPER PROFIT (LOSS) The unrealized difference between the current market price of a security and the price at which it was purchased.

PAR For common stock, it is the dollar amount assigned to shares when the company is formed. It is often $1.00 and has no relation to the market price. For preferred stock, the par is the value upon which dividends are figured. For a bond, the par value is the face amount, the amount due at maturity.

PAYOUT RATIO The percentage of a company's earnings which is paid out in dividends. It is computed by dividing dividends per share by earnings per share.

PORTFOLIO A list or collection of different investments owned.

PREMATURE DISTRIBUTIONS Employees who receive distributions from their 401(k) plan before they die, reach age 59½, are disabled, or retire after reaching age 55, can expect to pay a 10 percent penalty in addition to ordinary income tax on the distribution amount.

PRICE EARNINGS RATIO The PE ratio is computed by dividing the price of a stock by its earnings per share. The value of the ratio signifies how much in dollars an investor would pay to buy one dollar in earnings. All other things being equal, a lower PE means a "cheaper" stock.

PRIME RATE The rate charged by banks in lending to their most credit worthy customers.

PROSPECTUS A brochure containing legal and other information about a mutual fund or primary issue of securities. By law, it must be given to a potential customer by a broker before a purchase.

REAL RETURN The real return on an investment is its total return less the rate of inflation.

RECORD DATE The date on which a shareholder must be a registered owner of a company's stock in order to receive a declared dividend. The record date is four business days after the ex-dividend date.

ROLLOVER A rollover is a method of withdrawing funds from a 401(k) or 403(b) plan and reinvesting them with another custodian. In this procedure, the plan participant receives a check for the account value (or the actual stock or investments which were contained in the account) and then remits it to a new custodian. In order to avoid any income taxes or penalty, the funds must be remitted to the new custodian within sixty days of receipt. The IRS currently requires employers to withhold 20 percent of distributions which are paid directly to employees, even if the intent is to roll over the funds. See Chapter Nine for more detail on transfers and rollovers.

ROUND LOT Unit of trading or a multiple thereof. Generally 100 shares for common stocks and $1,000 or $5,000 par value for bonds.

SECURITIES AND EXCHANGE COMMISSION (SEC) An agency of the U.S. government established by the Securities Exchange Act of 1934 which requires full disclosure of financial information.

SELF-DIRECTED IRA An individual retirement arrangement which allows the purchase of investments from different issuers to be held in one account. For example, an investor may purchase common stock, corporate or U.S. Government bonds, and mutual funds all in one self-directed IRA.

SIPC The Securities Investor Protection Corporation insures the customers of member firms against fraud or failure of that firm.

STOCK DIVIDEND A dividend paid in securities rather than cash.

STOCK SPLIT An accounting function which increases the number of a company's outstanding shares of common stock. As no new value is added, the market price generally drops proportionately. An analogy for a two-for-one stock split is that it is the same as trading a dime for two nickels.

STREET NAME Securities which are held by a broker for a customer's account are held in the broker's name and said to be in street name.

TAX DEFERRAL Not paying income taxes on the growth or earnings of investments until you withdraw the money from a tax-protected account, such as a 401(k) or 403(b) plan, an IRA or an annuity.

TOTAL RETURN Income or dividends received plus the gain or loss of principal in the original investment equals total return.

TRANSFER Also called a direct transfer, or custodian to custodian transfer, this is a method of withdrawing your funds from your 401(k) plan and depositing them with another custodian. In a transfer, the funds are sent directly to the new custodian and never to the participant. The destination may be the custodian of an IRA, 401(k) plan, 403(b) plan, or any other qualified retirement plan. Transferring an account to another custodian prevents any current tax liability or IRS penalty.

TRANSFER AGENT The company which keeps a record of all registered shareholders, and sees that shares which are sold are properly canceled and that shares which are purchased are properly issued.

VESTING Employers have the option of rewarding length of employment by creating a schedule in which matching funds are "vested" after a certain number of years. Vested funds are yours and may be withdrawn, subject to the same restrictions as contributed funds. Funds which are not yet vested cannot be withdrawn.

YIELD-TO-MATURITY The yield figure of a bond which takes into account not only the interest payments, but the price discount or premium which was paid at purchase. A bond trading at a discount will have a yield to maturity that is higher than its current yield and a bond trading at a premium will have a yield to maturity that is lower than its current yield.

Index

About the Authors

Ellie Williams Clinton *(right)* graduated *summa cum laude* in Finance from the University of Missouri-Columbia. She has 10 years of banking and brokerage experience and managed a St. Louis brokerage firm. She is an experienced investment advisor and holds six securities licenses.

Diane Pearl graduated with an Associate of Science degree from Lake Land College in Mattoon, IL. As investment club director for a St. Louis bank, she provided training and education for many investment clubs. She acquired her interest in financial education during her years as a securities broker and holds four securities licenses.

Diane and Ellie are partners in *MONEYWISE,* a St. Louis based financial training and education firm dedicated to teaching people the right questions to ask and helping them make educated financial decisions. *MONEY-WISE* provides educational programs through the work place, to teach employees how to make the most of their paycheck, and how to make company benefit plans work for them.